Lexical Choices in English Translations of Chinese Novels:
A Corpus-driven Study

汉译英小说词汇文体研究

吴建 张韵菲 著

北京师范大学出版集团
BEIJING NORMAL UNIVERSITY PUBLISHING GROUP
安徽大学出版社

图书在版编目(CIP)数据

汉译英小说词汇文体研究 / 吴建，张韵菲著 . —合肥：安徽大学出版社，2021.12
ISBN 978-7-5664-2336-8

Ⅰ．①汉… Ⅱ．①吴… ②张… Ⅲ．①小说—英语—文学翻译—研究—中国 Ⅳ．① H315.9 ② I207.4

中国版本图书馆 CIP 数据核字(2021)第 254370 号

汉译英小说词汇文体研究
Hanyiying Xiaoshuo Cihui Wenti Yanjiu

吴　建　张韵菲　著

出版发行：	北京师范大学出版集团	
	安 徽 大 学 出 版 社	
	（安徽省合肥市肥西路3号 邮编230039）	
	www.bnupg.com.cn	
	www.ahupress.com.cn	
印　　　刷：	安徽利民印务有限公司	
经　　　销：	全国新华书店	
开　　　本：	170mm×240mm	
印　　　张：	12.25	
字　　　数：	238 千字	
版　　　次：	2021 年 12 月第 1 版	
印　　　次：	2021 年 12 月第 1 次印刷	
定　　　价：	46.00 元	

ISBN 978-7-5664-2336-8

策划编辑：李　梅　李　雪　　　　责任印制：赵明炎
责任编辑：李　雪　　　　　　　　装帧设计：李　军
责任校对：高婷婷　　　　　　　　美术编辑：李　军

版权所有　侵权必究

反盗版、侵权举报电话：0551-65106311
外埠邮购电话：0551-65107716
本书如有印装质量问题，请与印制管理部联系调换。
印制管理部电话：0551-65106311

前　言

中华文明共经历了4次翻译浪潮：汉唐的佛经东渐，明清的科技翻译大潮，"五四"时期以翻译为重要载体的新文化运动，以及如今我们正置身其中的新一波翻译大潮。在前3次翻译浪潮中，我们积极主动地将西方的思想文化精华引入中国。如今，我们希望把文化瑰宝送上世界舞台，尤其是展现在西方读者的面前。

虽然莫言在2012年12月8日成为了第一位荣膺诺贝尔文学奖的中国作家，但也难以掩盖中国文学西行路上的挫折。从20世纪80年代的"熊猫丛书"到90年代的"大中华文库"，再到近年的"中国文学海外传播项目"，种种努力，无不投入了大量人力和物力，可成效却并不喜人。目前在美国出版的外国文学作品中，中国作品仅占5%左右。可见，在世界文学的图景中，中国文学处于边缘状态。

中国文学出海艰难，背后的因素复杂多样。学界群策群力，在作品选择、出版渠道、宣传途径等宏观因素上着力探索。而笔者认为，对于中国文学走出去，或许最大、最值得研究的变量，非翻译莫属。翻译不好，再优秀的作品也难以有效传播。而好的翻译到底该是什么样子？这正是本书要回答的核心问题。

他山之石，可以攻玉。本书通过语料库方法细致分析了若干成功的母语译者译本在词汇语域、动词、名词、形容词、副词、代词、情态动词、介词、连词，以及词汇搭配等方面的文体特征。基于定量的统计与定性的分析后，我们发现，相对于非母语译者译本，母语译者译本总体上有以下特征：词汇使用更加丰富；词汇文体更加正式；词汇情感意义更为丰富；更偏爱抽象表达；更倾向避免词汇重复；相对偏好使用描写类词汇；语篇衔接方式更为紧凑；语言特征更能体现英语思维；更偏好超常表达；翻译策略更加灵活。

我们推测，母语译者与非母语译者在词汇运用上呈现上述差异，其原因除了在于译者个人风格,还在于各自母语思维的特性。母语译者的词汇选择更接近地道的英语思维,也更具创造性。

笔者希望本书能对汉语小说在英语世界的传播有所助益。不过,笔者才疏学浅,能力与精力有限,难免有疏漏与不足:第一,研究样本有限。书中所涉语料为5本汉语小说的母语译者与非母语译者翻译的英译本,语料达百万字词规模,在某种程度上能够支撑研究结论。不过,若有更大规模的语料,研究结论或会更有说服力。第二,研究维度有限。本书重点考察词汇维度,覆盖了几类主要词性及部分词汇搭配,揭示了母语译者译本若干词汇文体特征。研究并未涉及句法等更高层级的语法形式,也没有系统探索语篇衔接、叙事等文体维度。笔者希望,将来在理论、语料与工具更为成熟的条件下,能够开展维度更为丰富的比较研究。

本研究受到教育部人文社会科学基金项目"汉语小说英译母语—非母语译者词汇使用对比研究"(17YJC740094)的资助。

吴 建

2021年6月

目 录

第一章 研究概要 1
　一、研究缘起 1
　二、研究目标 1
　三、研究现状 2
　四、研究内容 4
　五、研究思路 5
　六、研究方法 5

第二章 词汇语域 6
　一、语域的概念 6
　二、词汇语域的定量分析 7
　三、词汇语域的定性分析 12
　本章小结 19

第三章 动词使用对比 21
　一、动词整体分布统计对比 21
　二、鲁迅小说两译本动词对比 22
　本章小结 33

第四章 名词使用对比 34
　一、总体名词对比 34
　二、抽象名词 35
　三、名词复现 45
　本章小结 48

第五章　形容词使用对比·················49
一、形容词使用总体特征·················50
二、强调性形容词·················51
三、形容词情感色彩对比·················57
四、描写性形容词·················63
五、最高级形容词·················66
本章小结·················80

第六章　副词使用对比·················82
一、副词整体特征·················82
二、程度副词·················83
三、方式副词·················98
四、否定副词·················100
本章小结·················102

第七章　代词使用对比·················103
一、反身代词·················103
二、指示代词·················107
本章小结·················114

第八章　情态动词使用对比·················115
一、情态动词总体对比·················115
二、鲁迅小说蓝译本与杨译本情态动词使用对比分析·················119
本章小结·················134

第九章　介词与连词使用对比·················136
一、介词·················137
二、连词·················140
本章小结·················153

第十章　词汇搭配 154
　一、副动搭配 154
　二、量名搭配 162
　三、N of N 搭配 165
　本章小结 171

结　语 173
　一、研究发现 173
　二、差异背后的可能原因 176
　三、研究价值 176
　四、研究的局限 176

参考文献 178
后　记 185

第一章　研究概要

一、研究缘起

汉语小说若想走进英语世界,其英译文语言的文学性至关重要(赵彦春 2019;孙会军 2018)。目前学界对汉译英小说的微观语言肌理重视不够。本研究以语料库为辅助手段,系统比较汉译英小说母语为英语的译者(以下简称"母语译者")与母语为汉语的译者(以下简称"非母语译者")的词汇使用特征,以此衡量译本的文学价值,从微观文体层面呼应中国文学走向海外这一时代命题。

二、研究目标

粗略而言,文学语言从文体意义的角度来看,有两种文体形式:一种是显性文体,以英语文学语言为典型;一种是隐性文体,以汉语文学语言为代表。当评估从显性文体到隐性文体的文学翻译时,应该采用原文文体导向型评估方式;而当评估从隐性文体到显性文体的文学翻译时,则更适合采用译文文体导向型评估方式(吴建 2017)。所谓原文文体导向型评估方式,重在考察原文显性文体表征在译文中的忠实传递;而所谓译文文体导向型评估方式,则衡量译文直接面对原文文体意义而作的创造性再现。当前学界在评估汉语小说英译时,主要采用原文文体导向型评估方式,对后一种模式重视不够。

本研究将采用译文文体导向型评估方式,对母语和非母语两种译者汉语小说英译的词汇层面进行定量为主、定性为辅的系统研究。课题目标分为理论目标和应用目标。理论上,丰富文学翻译的文体学视角研究,尤其丰富汉语小说英译的文体研究。应用上，为汉语小说英译提供词汇层面的评估尺度，也为其从业者提升译文质量、增强传播效果提供实际的参考依据。

三、研究现状

(一)基于语料库的汉语小说英译研究现状

语料库翻译学指采用语料库方法，在观察大量翻译事实或翻译现象并进行相关数据统计的基础上，系统分析翻译本质和翻译过程的研究(胡开宝 2012)。语料库翻译学研究发轫于 Baker(1993)，迄今已经形成了"一种连贯的、全面而丰富的研究范式……业已成为当代描写性译学研究的新范式(Laviosa，1998)"。汉语小说英译研究主体为中国学者，其他国家或地区寥寥无几。研究类型主要分为以下几块。

1. 翻译语言特征研究

翻译语言特征研究包括翻译共性研究和翻译文本特征实证研究。翻译共性亦称翻译普遍性或翻译普遍共性研究。Baker(1993)将其视为翻译本身固有的典型特征，主要关注翻译文本的以下共性：简化、显化、隐化、范化和整齐化。另有一些其他假设，如 Tirkkonen(2004)提出的"译入语独特性降低假设"等。在翻译共性研究中，国内学者最关注显化研究(宋庆伟等，2013)，且以英汉翻译为主要研究对象，如王克非、胡显耀(2010)、戴光荣、肖忠华(2010)、胡显耀(2010)、刘泽权、侯羽(2008)等。翻译文本特征实证研究对象亦以英译汉为主，研究内容涵盖词汇(胡显耀、曾佳，2010；王青、秦洪武，2011)、搭配(武光军、王克非，2011；肖忠华、戴光荣，2010)、句法(秦洪武、王克非，2004；秦洪武，2010；胡显耀、曾佳，2009)等方面。相对而言，以汉语小说英译为对象的研究较少，如姚琴(2013，《红楼梦》)、缪佳、邵斌(2014，《兄弟》)以及李珊妮、贾卉(2016，《受活》)等。

2. 译者风格研究

译者风格是"留在文本中的一系列语言和非语言的个性特征"(Baker 2000)，是指译者在语言应用方面所表现出的典型特征以及包括作为翻译对象的文本选择、翻译策略与方法的选用、前言、后记和译注等在内的非语言特征（胡开宝 2012）。基于语料库的译者风格定量分析大致涵盖词汇、词语搭配、句子、语篇等。词汇层面研究对象主要包括独特词、高频词、标准类符形符比、主题词、特殊词汇；词语搭配研究对象包括习语、词块、语义韵；句子层面研究对象涵盖句子数和平均句长、语态、汉英句子翻译对应类型等；语篇层面研究对象涵盖叙事标记语、语篇推进等；此外还有少数其他类型研究。就汉语小说英译领域而言，研究对象以明清小说及其译者为多，主要有：《红楼梦》：冯庆华（2008、2012，霍克斯译本）、刘泽权等（2011，四译本）、赵朝永（2014，邦斯尔译本）；《水浒传》：董琇（2009，赛珍珠译本）、刘克强（2013，四译本）；《聊斋志异》：卢静（2013，闵福德译本）；《浮生六记》：刘璇（2014，林语堂译本）；针对现当代作品英译的研究主要有：候羽等（2014，莫言等作家作品）；黄立波（2014，《骆驼祥子》）；王瑞、黄立波（2015，贾平凹作品）；李雅轩（2014，《红高粱》）；司炳月、霍跃红（2014，《尘埃落定》）；彭发胜（2014，《边城》）；严苡丹、韩宁（2015，鲁迅作品）等。

3. 具体问题研究

为数不少的研究借助语料库从微观层面对汉语小说英译中的具体问题做了定量研究。针对汉语古典小说的主要研究有：刘泽权、田璐（2009）对《红楼梦》中叙事标记语的英译做了定量分析；刘泽权、闫继苗（2010）对《红楼梦》中的报道动词及其英译做了定量分析；刘泽权、张丹丹（2012）从辞典编撰角度对《红楼梦》中和"吃"相关的熟语的英译做了统计研究；陈琳（2015）对《红楼梦》中的说书套语的英译做了定量分析；严苡丹（2011, 2012）对《红楼梦》中亲属称谓语的英译做了定量分析；谭业升（2013）对《红楼梦》英译中的"面子"话语做了定量研究；秦静、任晓霏（2015）从人物刻画视角对《红楼梦》中主述位结构做了统计研究；傅悦（2014）也从人物刻画视角对《红楼梦》英译本中的人物话语做了统计研究；杨柳川（2014）对《红楼梦》霍克斯译本中表颜色的词"红"的英译策略做了定量研究。针对现当代作品的主要研究有：朱冬青（2014）从语义韵视角对《狂人日记》三译本做了定量对比研究；黄立波（2011）从叙事视角出发对《骆驼祥子》英译本中的人称代词主语做了定量研究；王磊(2007)对《围城》英译本中的隐喻专门做了统计研究；熊丹等(2015)对明清小说英译中的人名称谓做了定量研究等。另有个别方法论上的研究，如黄立波(2013)对中国现当代小说汉英平行语料库研制与应用的探讨。

(二)现有研究的不足

1. 基于原文文体视角的研究有余，对译文文体关注不足

目前研究的主流视角是从原文文体出发，研究其在译文中的传达与再现，但针对译文文体的研究略显欠缺，而这种"再创作"视角的研究、对译文质量及其在译语读者中传播效果的关注在某种程度上更有现实意义，因为其对汉语小说更有效地走入英语世界这一时代命题有着十分重要的现实价值。

2. 对不同译者模式之间的文体差异对比不够系统

粗略而言，汉语小说英译有3种译者模式：母语译者模式；非母语译者模式；两者合作模式。此前研究对不同译者模式，尤其是母语与非母语译者模式之间的文体对比意识不强，对比不够系统。

3. 对数据挖掘及分析欠缺深度和系统性

欠缺深度表现在相当一部分研究止步于较为简单的数据统计以及对统计结果的笼统分析，以致于不少定量研究看似严谨，实则千篇一律，不能深入说明问题，违背了研究的宗旨。欠缺系统性表现在现有研究有相当一部分较为松散，针对某一个或多个语言层级进行的系统性定量研究较为少见。以词汇层级为例，很多定量研究只涉及形符比等少数几个方面。

四、研究内容

本研究以译文文体为导向，用定量为主、定性为辅的方法，对比母语译者的作品和非母语译者的作品(主要考察《红楼梦》《聊斋志异》、鲁迅小说、《浮生六记》《骆驼祥子》等作品的英译本)，在词汇使用层面的特征进行系统的描写与评估，揭示两种译者模式之间的差异，并总结高质量译文(在英语世界接受范围广、接受效果好的译文)的词汇使用特征。

五、研究思路

（一）语料库建设

本项目建设了 200 万单词以上规模的语料库。语料库所选译者及译本具有代表性，且每部作品皆有母语译者译本和非母语译者译本，以形成有效对比。

（二）数据挖掘

通过软件自动检索和手工检索，按照既定研究内容对语料库进行单语或平行检索、统计，得出初步数据。

（三）数据分析

对检索结果进行进一步分析，形成客观、系统的结论。

（四）提升总结

对结论进行定性总结，进一步形成评估性报告，并在此基础上提出相关建议。

（五）形成成果

相关报告与建议以若干篇论文以及一部专著的形式呈现。

六、研究方法

（一）基于语料库的定量检索

研究工具主要包括 Treetagger 等标注工具以及 Wordsmith、Antconc、CUC_paraconc 等检索工具。

（二）定量研究基础上的定性完善、分析与总结

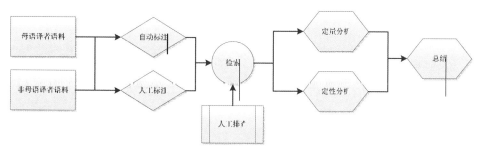

图 1.1 研究方法示意图

第二章 词汇语域

一、语域的概念

语域指的是适用于特定语境的语言变体。具体来说,语域就是在特定语境中,针对特定的交际对象,以特定的交际方式,为特定的交际目的而选择的特定的语言表达方式(曹明伦,2007)。卡特·福德在论及翻译中的语言变体时特意强调:语言变体大致分为永久性和临时性两类。前一类与说话人惯用的方言习语等永久性特点有关;后一类与说话人说话时所扮演的社会角色有关。与说话人说话时所扮演的社会角色有关的语言变体就被称为"语域"(Catford, 1965: 84-85)。

语言使用的领域种类繁多,有文学、新闻、演说、广告、科普、口语等。在不同领域使用的语言则形成不同的语言变体。应注意区分不同的语言变体,如具有某种具体用途的语言变体,与社会或区域(因说话者的不同而异)相对,是语言行为适应于某一特定活动类型、正式程度等的一种倾向。语域是由多种情境特征——特别是指语篇语场、语篇方式和语篇基调——相联系的语言特征构成的。语域是语篇针对特定的交际场合,为达到某一交际目的而产生的一种功能变体,是多种参数——语篇语场、方式和基调——的综合体现,不只是一种单纯的语篇方式变体。

汉语是一种语域包容性极强的语言,至少比英语的语域包容性更强。由于英语重形合,汉语重意合,故英语的语域变化主要发生在语法层面,而汉语的语域变化则主要体现在词汇层面。

二、词汇语域的定量分析

本研究选定五个文本的母语译者译本与非母语译者译本作为研究对象,分别为《浮生六记》的拜伦译本与林语堂译本(以下简称"林译本"),《红楼梦》(21-30章)的霍克斯译本与杨宪益、戴乃迭译本(以下简称"霍译本"与"杨译本"),《骆驼祥子》的葛浩文译本与施晓菁译本(以下简称"葛译本"与"施译本"),鲁迅小说的蓝诗玲译本与杨宪益、戴乃迭译本(以下简称"蓝译本"与"杨译本"),《聊斋志异》的闵福德译本(以下简称"闵译本")与大中华译本。定量研究部分主要统计几对译本在词汇使用的词类数量(即类符数)、标准类符形符比、词长、句长4个指标。其中,词类数量与标准类符形符比显示译本的词汇丰富程度,而词长与句长则昭示译本的正式程度。具体统计数字如表2.1和表2.2所示。

表2.1 母语、非母语译者词汇使用统计表

原著	《浮生六记》	《红楼梦》(21-30章)	《骆驼祥子》	鲁迅小说	《聊斋志异》	合计
非母语译者译本	林译本	杨译本	施译本	杨译本	大中华译本	
形符	46135	49630	89323	97549	60368	343005
类符	4959	5418	7815	7927	5475	15740
标准类符形符比	42.4	44.67	43.67	43.14	41.51	43.11
词长	4.1	4.2	4.24	4.21	4.19	4.2
句均词	22.87	12.96	14.53	15.03	14.54	15.15
母语译者译本	拜伦译本	霍译本	葛译本	蓝译本	闵译本	
形符	46629	69939	94522	92451	65776	369317
类符	4600	6847	8111	9473	6606	18038

（续表）

母语译者译本	拜伦译本	霍译本	葛译本	蓝译本	闵译本	
标准类符形符比	41.13	42.66	43.61	46.5	43.41	43.81
词长	4.04	4.18	4.25	4.35	4.22	4.23
句均词	19.07	16.15	15.04	15.83	17.16	16.24

（一）标准类符型符比

除鲁迅小说以外，其他4对译本中，母语译者译本词汇数量（即形符数）均超过非母语译者译本，其中，《红楼梦》两译本差距最大，这和两译本参考的底本有一定的关系。从词类数量（即类符数）来看，大多数母语译者使用了比非母语译者更多的词类。这在某种程度上表明，母语译者的词汇使用更加丰富。值得注意的是，《浮生六记》的非母语译者林语堂使用了比母语译者拜伦更丰富的词汇。

（二）平均词长与句长

基于平均词长来看，《浮生六记》《红楼梦》的非母语译者译本长于母语译者译本，而《骆驼祥子》、鲁迅小说以及《聊斋志异》的3对译本中，母语译者译本平均词长更长。

从平均句长来看，除了《浮生六记》，其他几对译本中，母语译者译本均较非母语译者译本句子更长，其中《红楼梦》译本差距最明显。这在某种程度上表明，母语译者译本的句式可能更为复杂。

（三）各长度单词分布情况

根据下表各译本单词长度分布数据来看，在母语译者译本与非母语译者译本中，各长度单词占总词数的比重基本一致，二者也符合英语原著语料库中各长度单词使用的统计情况。

母语译者译本与非母语译者译本在不同长度单词的分布上呈现出细微却具有系统性的差异。五对译本对比数据平均值显示，在非母语译者译本中，长度为3、4、5、6字母的单词占比高于母语译者译本，而其他长度的单词占比低于母语译者译本。在非母语译者译本中，1字母长度的单词占总词数比重为3.8%，低于母语译者译本4.11%，两者相差0.31%；非母语译者译本2字母长度单词占比为17.03%，比母语译者译本的16.67%低0.36%。3字母、4字母、5字母、6字母长度单词占比，非母语译者译本均高于母语译者译本，分别高出0.3%、0.48%、0.67%、0.17%；7字母、8字母、9字母、10字母以及10字母以上长度单词的占比数据呈现相反的态势，母语译者译本分别高出非母语译者译本0.11%、0.15%、0.19%、0.2%和0.14%。

各译本的数据与平均数据并不完全相符，《红楼梦》两译本符合度为73%，母语译者译本中的3字母长度单词占比高于非母语译者译本，而7字母、8字母长度单词占比却低于非母语译者译本。《骆驼祥子》两译本符合度为64%，其中有4处与平均数据不符：母语译者译本中的2字母、7字母和9字母长度单词占比低于非母语译者译本，4字母长度单词占比高于非母语译者译本；鲁迅小说译本符合度为82%，其中有2处不符合，2字母长度单词使用比例非母语译者译本高出母语译者译本，6字母长度单词则相反；《聊斋志异》译本符合度为100%。《浮生六记》两译本符合度最低，只有9%，在11项不同长度单词的对比中，只有6字母长度单词与平均数据相符，这从某种程度上说明，相较而言，林译本在语域层面十分接近母语译者译本的总体词汇特征。

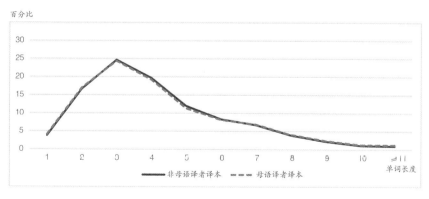

图2.1 母语、非母语译者译本各长度单词使用分布对比图

表 2.2 母语、非母语译者译本单词长度统计表

原著	词长	1	2	3	4	5	6	7	8	9	10	11	12	13	14	15	16	17	18	19	20	21	22
《浮生六记》	非母语译者译本	2861	8227	10580	8612	5538	3756	2797	1771	1038	514	247	99	60	26	9	0	0	0	0	0	0	0
	%	6.2	17.83	22.93	18.67	12	8.14	6.06	3.84	2.25	1.11						0.96						
	母语译者译本	2835	8309	10908	9182	5608	3631	2675	1696	923	483	222	95	49	12	0	1	0	0	0	0	0	0
	%	6.08	16.84	23.39	19.69	12.03	7.79	5.74	3.64	1.98	1.04						0.81						
《红楼梦》（21-30章）	非母语译者译本	1472	7853	12491	10280	6293	4214	3325	1926	965	468	197	98	41	3	4	0	0	0	0	0	0	0
	%	2.97	15.82	25.17	20.71	12.68	8.49	6.7	3.88	1.94	0.94						0.69						
	母语译者译本	2226	12192	17976	14243	7528	5352	4573	2551	1616	810	506	218	97	30	15	6	0	0	0	0	0	0
	%	3.18	17.43	25.7	20.36	10.76	7.65	6.54	3.65	2.31	1.16						1.25						
《骆驼祥子》	非母语译者译本	2518	15206	22342	16967	10777	7430	6838	3606	1926	948	393	219	80	32	21	7	7	1	2	1	2	0
	%	2.82	17.02	25.01	19	12.07	8.32	7.65	4.04	2.15	1.06						0.85						
	母语译者译本	2874	16056	23550	18031	11238	7786	6889	4021	1981	1084	536	253	113	49	27	11	6	5	8	2	1	0
	%	3.04	16.98	24.91	19.07	11.89	8.24	7.29	4.25	2.1	1.15						1.07						
鲁迅小说	非母语译者译本	4219	16340	23161	19497	11543	8081	6277	3759	2342	1233	562	304	140	50	39	1	1	0	0	0	0	0
	%	4.33	16.75	23.74	19.9	11.83	8.28	6.43	3.85	2.4	1.26						1.12						
	母语译者译本	4879	15362	20281	16932	10434	7914	6712	4162	2618	1582	812	430	188	91	33	10	4	3	0	0	2	2
	%	5.28	16.62	21.94	18.31	11.29	8.56	7.26	4.5	2.83	1.71						1.7						

第二章　词汇语域

（续表）

原著	词长	1	2	3	4	5	6	7	8	9	10	11	12	13	14	15	16	17	18	19	20	21	22
《聊斋志异》	非母语译者译本	1983	9537	15903	12116	7140	5029	3851	2371	1341	573	311	140	55	9	7	1	0	0	0	0	0	1
	%	3.28	15.8	26.34	20.1	11.85	8.3	6.34	3.93	2.22	0.95						0.87						
	母语译者译本	2378	10958	17138	12466	7171	5374	4404	2594	1772	811	403	191	81	19	9	3	4	0	0	0	0	0
	%	3.62	16.66	26.06	18.95	10.9	8.17	6.7	3.94	2.69	1.23						1.08						
合计	非母语译者译本	13053	57163	84477	67472	41291	28510	23088	13433	7612	3736	1710	860	376	120	80	9	8	1	2	1	2	1
	%	3.8	16.67	24.63	19.67	12.04	8.31	6.73	3.92	2.22	1.09						0.93						
	母语译者译本	15192	62877	89853	70854	41979	30057	25253	15024	8910	4770	2479	1187	528	201	84	31	14	8	8	2	3	2
	%	4.11	17.03	24.33	19.19	11.37	8.14	6.84	4.07	2.41	1.29						1.22						
	原著	87895	345953	481353	367826	214825	158264	123508	76633	54815	29829						28442						
	%	4.45	17.56	24.44	18.68	10.91	8.03	6.27	3.89	2.78	1.51						1.44						

三、词汇语域的定性分析

（一）词汇正式度

词汇的正式度是语域的重要方面，也是译者风格的重要指标。我们以《聊斋志异》的闵译本和大中华译本为例，比较两译本的词汇正式度。我们聚焦4类词性：动词、名词、形容词与副词。先从数据上比较4类词性各长度单词在译本中的分布，之后再各举出2处译文作为示例。

1. 动词对比

表2.3 《聊斋志异》两译本各长度动词分布

词长 译本	1	2	3	4	5	6	7	8	9	10	11+	合计
大中华译本	-	211	904	2620	1434	1569	1443	756	432	166	91	9626
%	-	2.19	9.39	27.22	14.90	16.30	15	7.85	4.49	1.72	0.94	100%
闵译本	-	186	741	2335	1356	1461	1581	1045	686	256	158	9805
%	-	1.89	7.56	23.81	13.83	14.91	16.12	10.66	6.99	2.61	1.61	100%

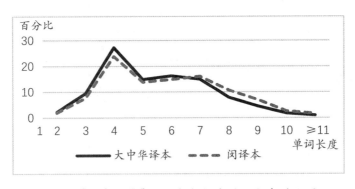

图2.2 《聊斋志异》两译本各长度动词分布对比图

可以看出，在2~6个字母组成的动词数量上，大中华译本的绝对数量与占比均高于闵译本，而在7个以上字母组成的动词数量上，闵译本则均高于大中华译本。这说明，相比较而言，闵译本中的动词更长，也因此更为正式。

原文：一官绅在扬州买妾，连相数家，悉不当意。

大中华译本：A man was trying to buy a concubine in Yangzhou. He **visited** several families and found no girls to his liking.

闵译本：A wealthy gentleman of Yangzhou wanted to buy himself a concubine. He had **inspected** several women but found that none of them was really what he was looking for.

原文中的动词"相"，大中华译本中译为 visit，闵译本 inspect，两相比较，后者更为正式。

原文：至夜入衾，肤腻如脂。喜扪私处，则男子也。

大中华译本：At night, under the quilt, the man found the girl's skin creamy smooth. He touched her lower parts and was astonished to **find** that his new concubine was actually a boy.

闵译本：The very first night they slept together, he admired the silken softness of her skin and proceeded in a transport of delight to explore her private parts, when to his shock and horror he **discovered** that "she" was in fact a boy.

原文中的"喜扪私处，则男子也"，省略了动词"发现"。该动词在大中华译本中译为 find，与闵译本中的 discover 相比，后者语域相对正式。

2. 名词对比

表 2.4 《聊斋志异》两译本各长度名词分布

译本\词长	1	2	3	4	5	6	7	8	9	10	≥11	合计
大中华译本	-	173	1283	2591	2375	1885	1071	734	433	202	222	10969
%	-	1.58	11.70	23.62	21.65	17.18	9.76	6.69	3.95	1.84	2.02	100
闵译本	-	175	1413	2737	2399	1948	1195	771	547	254	298	11737
%	-	1.49	12.04	23.32	20.44	16.60	10.18	6.57	4.66	2.16	2.54	100

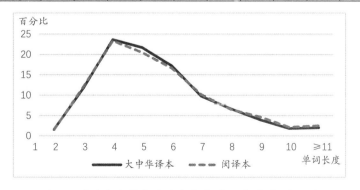

图 2.3 《聊斋志异》两译本各长度名词分布对比图

从上表看,各长度名词的分布与动词的分布略有不同。从各长度名词在各自译本所占百分比来看,除了3字母组成的名词,在2~6字母组成的名词中,大中华译本占比均高于闵译本,而在7个以上字母组成的名词中,除去8字母长度的名词,闵译本均高于大中华译本。整体而言,闵译本在名词的使用方面较大中华译本更为正式。以下是两个译例。

原文:审视之,咽不断者盈指。

大中华译本:The family members took a careful **look** and found that the head was still linked to the body by the throat.

闵译本:…they detected the faintest trace of breathing, and on closer **examination** saw that the man's windpipe was not quite severed.

原文中的"审视"对应两个名词 look 和 examination,两者相比,后者更为正式。

原文:渐至白昼宣淫……

大中华译本:Often he would have **sex** with the maids, sometimes even during daytime…

闵译本:One thing led to another, and soon they were indulging in full-blown **intercourse** in broad daylight.

闵译本中的 intercourse 比大中华译本中的 sex 更加正式。

3. 形容词对比

表2.5 《聊斋志异》两译本各长度形容词分布

译本\词长	1	2	3	4	5	6	7	8	9	10	≥11	合计
大中华译本	-	-	365	799	721	423	341	226	152	75	61	3163
%	-	-	11.54	25.26	22.79	13.37	10.78	7.15	4.81	2.37	1.93	100
闵译本	-	-	377	797	822	564	445	270	210	89	109	3683
%	-	-	10.24	21.64	22.32	15.31	12.08	7.33	5.70	2.42	2.96	100

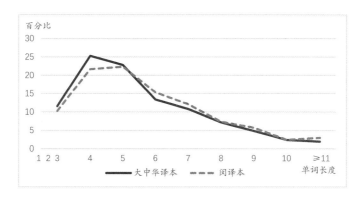

图 2.4 《聊斋志异》两译本各长度形容词分布图

可以看出，在 2~5 个字母组成的形容词中，大中华译本的绝对数量与占比均高于闵译本，而在 6 个以上字母组成的动词中，闵译本则均高于大中华译本。这说明，闵译本中的形容词更长，也因此更为正式。看两个例子。

原文：以匕箸稍哺饮食。

大中华译本：…the family members fed him a **little** food with chopsticks and a spoon.

闵译本：They fed him **minute** quantities of food with a spoon and chopsticks.

大中华译本中的 little 不如闵译本中的 minute 正式。

原文：无何，宁妻亡。

大中华译本：**Soon**, Ning's wife passed away.

闵译本：After a **considerable** interval of time, Ning's wife died.

闵译本中使用了较为正式的形容词 considerable。

4. 副词对比

表 2.6 《聊斋志异》两译本各长度副词分布

译本＼词长	1	2	3	4	5	6	7	8	9	10	≥11	合计
大中华译本	-	370	557	1296	634	270	245	169	116	67	90	3814
%	-	9.70	14.60	33.98	16.62	7.08	6.42	4.43	3.04	1.76	2.36	100
闵译本	-	307	638	1121	657	348	363	224	175	138	121	4092
%	-	7.50	15.59	27.39	16.06	8.50	8.87	5.47	4.28	3.37	2.96	100

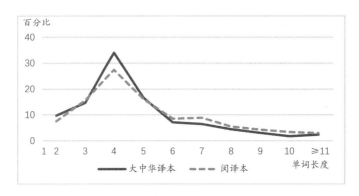

图2.5《聊斋志异》两译本各长度副词分布对比图

从各长度副词在各自译本所占百分比来看，除了3字母组成的副词，在2~6字母组成的副词中，大中华译本占比均高于闵译本，而在6个以上字母组成的副词中，闵译本则均高于大中华译本。就整体而言，闵译本在副词的使用较大中华译本正式。看两个译例。

原文：翁殊博洽，镂花雕缋，粲于牙齿……

大中华译本：The old man was **very** learned, citing classics and coming up with witty remarks.

闵译本：…his guest showed himself to be **extraordinarily** learned and eloquent, expressing himself most gracefully and expounding the classics with unusual insight.

大中华译本中的 very 不如闵译本中的 extraordinarily 正式。

原文：妪归，备道三娘容止，父母皆喜。

大中华译本：After she got back, the old woman gave a detailed description of Sanniang's looks and manners, which **quite** pleased the old couple.

闵译本：On her return, the matchmaker conveyed to Lian's parents her favourable impressions of Tertia, which pleased them **greatly**.

两译本中的 greatly 与 quite 都是程度副词，但前者属于较为正式的语体。

（二）词汇语域的人物刻画功能

语域具有十分丰富的文体价值。使用不同正式程度的语言描绘人物的语言与行为，可起到十分有效的人物刻画功能。在作为叙事文学代表的小说中尤为如此，因为人物是小说的主脑、核心和台柱（吴怀仁 2009）。在中国传统的文学理论看来，对一部小说评价的高低，往往取决于这部小说对其人物性格展现与揭示的程度（姜静楠 2000）。因此，人物塑造自然应成为译者主要关注的核心要素。叙事小说中人物塑造的方式多种多样，因此笔者难以一一总结。正如戴维·洛奇（David Lodge，1992）所言，人物可能是最难在技术层面上讨论的小说元素，因为人物类别纷繁复杂，呈现的方式也多种多样。但人物语言和行为应该是最重要的两个方面。下面，我们就以语域这一指标为抓手，聚焦鲁迅著名短篇小说《孔乙己》中的主人公孔乙己的刻画及其翻译，探讨不同正式程度的语言在人物的刻画中起到何种作用。

1. 孔乙己的语言

孔乙己是旧社会读书人，头脑中有旧观念，言辞亦故作深沉、迂腐不堪。且看下面两例。

原文：孔乙己着了慌，伸开五指将碟子罩住，弯腰下去说道，"不多了，我已经不多了。"直起身又看一看豆，自己摇头说，"不多不多！多乎哉？不多也。"

杨译本：Flustered, he would cover the dish with his hand and, bending forward from the waist, would say: **"There isn't much. I haven't much as it is."** Then straightening up to look at the peas again, he would shake his head. **"Not much! Verily, not much, forsooth!"**

蓝译本：**"Hardly any left,"** an unnerved Kong would scoop to tell them, his fingers sheltering the dish. Straightening up, he would glance back at the beans shaking his head: **"Hardly any! Are the beans multitudinous in abundance? Multitudinous in abundance they are not."**

孔乙己言辞陈腐气十足，即便在对孩子们说话时也不忘拽上两句之乎者也。这种让人物跃然纸上的话语，译者自然不该忽视。两位译者均试图加以再现，但相比之下，蓝译本用语更具文味，且没有放过原文中具有强烈喜剧色彩的自问自答"多乎哉？不多也"，较之杨译本更胜一筹。

2. 孔乙己的行为

话语之外，行为亦是人物刻画的一把关键钥匙。我们试着分析一下书中人物行为的描写，比较两位译者在翻译人物行为描写时的用语各有什么得失。

原文：我愈不耐烦了，努着嘴走远。孔乙己刚用指甲蘸了酒，想在柜上写字，见我毫不热心，便又叹一口气，显出极惋惜的样子。

杨译本：My patience exhausted, I scowled and made off. Kung I-chi had dipped his finger in wine, in order to trace the characters on the counter; but when he saw how indifferent I was, he sighed and looked most disappointed.

蓝译本：I walked off, scowling. Kong Yiji sighed—his fingernail already dipped in wine, ready to scrawl the characters across the bar—at my lamentable absence of academic zeal.

此处孔乙己对"我"的不热心露出失望、惋惜之情。杨译本如实译出原文信息，未增情趣。而蓝译本则用了很正式的语言，让读者更深切地感受到孔乙己的"迂腐"。这一细节暗合了贯穿全文的孔乙己旧文人的秉性。蓝译本这一特点在其译文中处处可见，其不仅着力表现孔乙己语言之迂腐，在描写孔乙己行为时也尽量用文绉绉的词语，让孔乙己的形象跃然纸上。

原文：孔乙己自己知道不能和他们谈天，便只好向孩子说话。

杨译本：Knowing it was no use talking to them, Kung would chat to us children.

蓝译本：Recognizing that he'd never **get the better of them**, Kong Yiji **concentrated his conversational efforts on** any minors he encountered about the premises.

蓝译本用幽默的语言表达了孔乙己干不过短衣帮，只好在小孩子身上找自信的心态。Could never get the better of them 很好地再现了孔乙己和短衣帮之间的"语言斗争"，concentrated his conversational efforts on 属于较为正式的句式，语言正式度和内容琐碎性之间的张力形成一种很好的喜剧效果，也和孔乙己人物话语的迂腐一脉相承，由喜衬悲。

原文：他便给他们茴香豆吃，一人一颗……孔乙己着了慌，伸开五指将碟子罩住，弯腰下去说道……

杨译本：Kung I-chi then he would give them peas flavoured with aniseed, one apiece... Flustered, he would **cover** the dish with his hand and, bending forward from the waist, would say...

蓝译本：He would present each with a single aniseed bean...an unnerved Kong would scoop to tell them, his fingers **sheltering** the dish.

"罩住"是很形象的词语。蓝译本的 shelter 较之杨译本的 cover 更能表现孔乙己"护豆"心切。另外，与上例同理，shelter 一词较之 cover 更加正式，既增添喜剧效果，也更符合孔乙己的迂腐形象。

本章小结

语域是重要的文体指标。本章对比了母语译者译本与非母语译者译本的语域特征，聚焦几对译本在词类数量、标准类符形符比、词长、句长 4 个指标方面的区别。研究得出以下结论。

（一）母语译者词汇使用更加丰富

总体而言，母语译者译本词汇数量均超过非母语译者译本，其中鲁迅小说两译本为例外。这在某种程度上说明，母语译者在信息传递方面更加详实。从词类数量来看，大多数母语译者使用了比非母语译者更多的词类，《红楼梦》、鲁迅小说以及《聊斋志异》的母语译者使用词汇类别比非母语译者均超出 1000，悬殊较大。《浮生六记》例外，它的林译本比拜伦译本多出 359 个词类。总体而言，母语译者词汇的使用更加丰富。

（二）母语译者译本词汇文体更加正式

从平均词长来看，总体而言，母语译者译本平均词长更长，这说明母语译者译本的语域相较于非母语译者译本而言，更加正式；从平均句长来看，母语译者译本均较非母语译者译本句子更长，这在某种程度上表明，母语译者译本的句式可能更为复杂。再从各长度单词分布情况来看，5 对译本对比数据平均值显示，非母语译者译本中，长度为 3、4、5、6 字母的单词占比高于母语译者译本，而其他长度的单词占比低于母语译者译本。这也进一步说明，母语译者译本的词汇正式度高于非母语译者译本。上述统计在以《聊斋志异》的闵译本和大中华译本为案例的分析中也得到了部分印证。

（三）语域蕴含着丰富的文体价值

在小说创作中，正式程度不同的语言描绘人物的语言与行为，可发挥十分有效的人物刻画功能。同样，在小说翻译中，语域的人物刻画功能也不容忽视。我们从鲁迅小说《孔乙己》蓝、杨译本的对比分析中，看到了两位译者在利用语域再现鲁迅笔下孔乙己人物形象方面的得与失。

第三章　动词使用对比

动词是重要词性，是叙事语言风格的重要构成，因此也是翻译，尤其是文学翻译风格的重点考察指标。我们利用语料库检索对两类译本中的动词使用进行了多个维度的统计与对比。本研究统计以实义动词为主。

一、动词整体分布统计对比

我们使用 Wordsmith 统计了各译本中动词的形符数、类符数与平均词长。具体如下表：

表 3.1 各译本动词统计对比

原著	译本	形符	类符	平均词长
鲁迅小说	蓝译本	14176	2650	5.54
	杨译本	13141	2991	5.79
《聊斋志异》	大中华译本	9714	1918	5.46
	闵译本	9839	2244	5.85
《骆驼祥子》	施译本	13352	2642	5.33
	葛译本	14321	2707	5.38
《红楼梦》（21-30 章）	杨译本	8312	1903	5.3
	霍译本	10633	2139	5.36
《浮生六记》	林译本	5755	1410	5.55
	拜伦译本	6303	1466	5.41

上表数据统计结果如下。从词符来看，5 对译本中，除了鲁迅小说的杨译本，其他非母语译者使用的动词数量均少于母语译者；差别最大者为《红楼梦》霍译本与杨译本。从词形来看，非母语译者使用的动词类型均少于母语译者，其中悬殊最大的为《聊斋志异》的闵译本与大中华译本，两者相差 398 个，差距十分显著；

悬殊最小的为《浮生六记》译本，两者相差 56 个。这说明母语译者译本的词汇丰富度普遍超过非母语译者译本。从平均词长这一指标来看，除了《浮生六记》的林译本，母语译者译本使用的动词词长均长于非母语译者译本，这反映了母语译者的用词正式度普遍高于非母语译者。上述统计在某种程度上说明了林语堂的翻译风格并非典型的非母语译者风格。

二、鲁迅小说两译本动词对比

(一) 动词使用统计对比

我们对鲁迅小说两译本做了更为精确的统计，在软件自动统计的基础上，人工剔除部分机器未能识别的重复与冗余，得到了更为可信的数据。蓝译本与杨译本在实义动词的数量上不相上下，蓝译本为 13319 个，杨译本为 13320 个，相差无几。但两个译本在实义动词类型上相差甚多，蓝译本为 1777 个，比杨译本的 1330 个动词类别高出 447 个。具体见表 3.2。这意味着，蓝译本的动词使用比杨译本要丰富得多。

表 3.2 蓝译本与杨译本动词总体统计

	蓝译本	杨译本
形符	13319	13320
类符	1777	1330

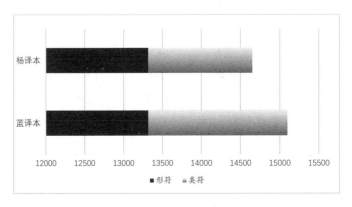

图 3.1 蓝译本与杨译本动词使用总体数据对比图

(二)各长度动词分布统计对比

单词长度是用词正式度的一个指标,也是语篇风格的风向标。在叙事体裁中,不同的词汇语域特征所对应的人物形象塑造效果也不同。我们在第二章的语域对比中对此做了较为详细的论述与例证。我们将鲁迅小说蓝译本与杨译本中各长度动词的分布做了详细的统计,见表3.3以及图3.2、图3.3。从动词类别统计上看,除了2字母与3字母长度的单词,蓝译本的动词类别均多于杨译本。从数量上来看,杨译本对2~5字母以及7字母长度的单词的使用多于蓝译本,而蓝译本更多使用正式度更高的动词。

表3.3 鲁迅小说蓝译本与杨译本动词长度分布统计

词长	蓝译本		杨译本	
	类符	形符	类符	形符
<2	0	0	0	0
2	2	661	2	1041
3	92	1045	99	1202
4	377	4754	337	5222
5	384	2655	338	3647
6	395	1657	313	1487
7	258	727	232	783
8	125	406	111	390
9	72	178	62	118
10	41	109	36	89
>10	29	63	14	17
Total				

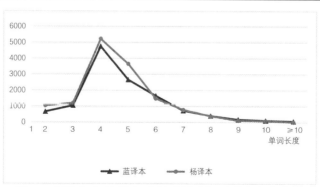

图3.2 蓝译本与杨译本动词数量(即形符)对比统计

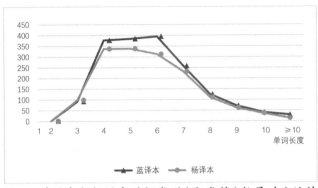

图 3.3 蓝译本与杨译本动词类型（即类符）数量对比统计

（三）高频词统计对比

我们将两译本排名前 50 的高频词统计对比，如下表所示。不难看出，杨译本前 50 高频词的平均数量较蓝译本高。杨译本前 50 高频词总数为 6910，平均每个单词出现频次为 138.2，蓝译本前 50 高频词总数为 5962，词均频次为 119.24，二者相差 18.96。

表 3.4 蓝译本与杨译本前 50 高频动词对比

	杨译本		蓝译本	
1	do	592	go	357
2	go	449	do	304
3	say	443	take	278
4	see	333	get	254
5	come	310	think	235
6	look	281	say	233
7	know	261	see	215
8	take	255	look	184
9	make	252	know	181
10	think	221	make	180
11	feel	169	come	180
12	ask	153	begin	157
13	give	150	tell	133
14	hear	139	leave	130
15	call	128	feel	125

（续表）

	杨译本		蓝译本	
16	want	125	turn	119
17	eat	123	give	119
18	seem	123	seem	115
19	tell	123	hear	115
20	turn	123	bring	110
31	get	122	sit	106
32	leave	120	ask	106
33	stand	120	find	102
34	put	95	want	101
35	find	94	fail	92
36	start	90	eat	84
37	become	89	try	82
38	use	81	stand	81
39	grow	78	keep	76
40	begin	77	set	74
41	keep	76	call	73
42	walk	73	hold	66
43	bring	72	return	62
44	let	70	lay	62
45	stop	69	remember	60
46	happen	63	follow	60
47	sit	61	walk	55
48	write	61	let	52
49	buy	60	use	50
50	live	56	start	50
合计		6910		5962
词均		138.2		119.24

前50高频词分布态势也反映整个译本动词使用分布特征。整体而言，杨译本高频词数量较多，词汇分布较为集中，而蓝译本则分布较平滑。如下图。

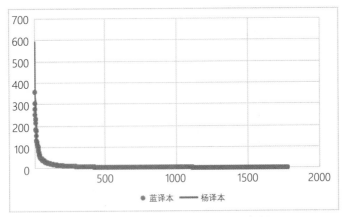

图 3.4 蓝译本与杨译本动词分布图

（四）独特动词统计对比

所谓独特动词，指某译本使用、但在对照译本未出现的动词。我们利用 Python 3.8 自然语言处理模块 nltk 工具包对蓝译本与杨译本相对于彼此的独特动词进行了提取和对比，并按照字母长度做了统计（见表 3.5）。统计发现，3 个字母长度的独特动词，杨译本的类别高于蓝译本，多出 4 个。而 3 个字母以上长度的动词，蓝译本所使用的词汇数量及类别均高于杨译本。这说明，蓝译本的动词使用较之杨译本更为丰富。

表 3.5 鲁迅小说两译本独特动词统计

词长	蓝译本		杨译本		对比
	类符	形符	类符	形符	
<3	0	0	0	0	0/0
3	23	48	27	42	6/6
4	94	185	61	81	33/104
5	104	189	58	80	46/109
6	163	278	81	118	82/160
7	38	48	14	17	24/31
8	56	83	46	64	10/19
9	39	57	27	35	12/22
10	17	30	11	13	6/17
>10	23	41	8	10	5/31
Total	557	959	333	460	224/499

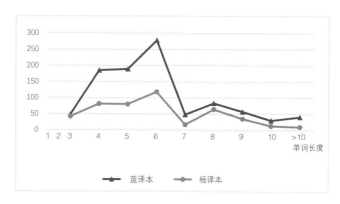

图 3.5 蓝译本与杨译本独特动词数量（即形符数）对比统计

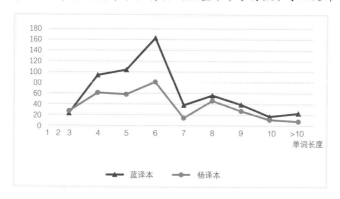

图 3.6 蓝译本与杨译本独特动词类型（即类符数）对比统计

（五）动词丰富性统计对比

本节我们以言说动词（speaking verbs）及感知动词（sensing verbs）为例，比较一下鲁迅小说两译本分别使用了多少以及何种动词，以此作为指标比较、衡量两译本动词使用的丰富程度。

1. 言说动词

我们先统计原文中的言说动词"说"，以及两译本最常见言说动词 say，speak，talk，tell 的使用频率。

表 3.6 蓝译本与杨译本常见言说动词英译统计

项目	原文	蓝译本	杨译本
说	882	0	0
say	0	233	443

（续表）

项目	原文	蓝译本	杨译本
speak	0	28	48
tell	0	134	125
talk	0	41	53
合计	882	436	669

从上表可以看出，鲁迅小说全文有882个"说"字（其中有少数并非典型的言说动词，如"听说"）。两译本中，蓝译本使用的四种常见言说动词案例为436个，杨译本为669个，前者比后者少了233个。这一数据对比说明，两译本均使用了大量其他动词表达原文言说动词，而相比之下，蓝译本使用数量更多。

为了更加深入了解两译本具体使用了何种动词，运用了何种翻译策略，我们聚焦《阿Q正传》蓝译本与杨译本中的具体译例。《阿Q正传》中一共出现动词"说"119次，其中107例表言说之意。总结下来，主要英译策略有以下几种：（1）对应，即say及其变体（says, said, saying）；（2）变换，指其他高频言说动词，如tell, speak, talk等；（3）显创，即显化或创造，指译文根据语境对原文进行显化处理或为了修辞效果进行"无中生有"的发挥创造，如使用bark等形象的下义词；（4）省略，即对利用语境信息进行相应的省略处理。见表3.7和3.8。

（1）对应

原文：他癞疮疤块块通红了，将衣服摔在地上，吐一口唾沫，说："这毛虫！"

杨译本：All Ah Q's scars turned scarlet. Flinging his jacket on the ground, he spat and **said**, "Hairy worm!"

（2）变换

原文：说是算被儿子拿去了罢，总还是忽忽不乐……

蓝译本：He tried **telling** himself his son had stolen it; his discontent continued to simmer.

（3）显创

原文：他走近柜台，从腰间伸出手来，满把是银的和铜的，在柜上一扔说，"现钱！打酒来！"

蓝译本：Walking up to the bar, he pulled from his belt a fistful of silver and copper coins. "Wine!" he **barked**, throwing them down. "I'm paying cash!"

（4）省略

原文："谁认便骂谁！"他站起来，两手叉在腰间说。

杨译本："Takes one to know one!" He stood up, hands on hips.

表 3.7 蓝译本与杨译本中言说动词"说"的英译详细情况

策略	蓝译本	杨译本
对应	say（1/17）	say（1/42）
变换	tell（1/10）	speak; talk; tell（3/12）
显创	add one's own revisions; ask（3）; bark; be forthcoming; chatter; claim; command; confess; counter; creep out; declare; demonstrate; echo; exclaim; falter; get sb's attention; hazard a guess; hear; insist; interject; interpolate; intone; keep on; learn; leave; mention; mumble; mutter; negotiate; observe; pant out; pluck...a line out of...; protest; put about（2）; be quick to mouth off about; quite simply; quote; rabble; refer to; remark（2）; repeat; reply（2）; report（2）; roar; shoot one's mouth off about...; sneer; spill; venture; view as taboo; with （48/54）	according to（4）; agree; answer（2）; ask（2）; be silent; boast; chatter; consider as; consider it tantamount to; declare; demand（3）; echo; exclaim（3）; explain; find; hiss; inform; maintain; make remarks; mutter; pant; pass remarks; protest（2）; put forward the hypothesis; put in; put in a few words; remark（2）; repeat（2）; reply; retort; shout; to tell the truth; use the word; utter（2）; words slip out （35/44）
省略	omitted（1/22）	omitted（1/7）

表 3.8 蓝译本与杨译本言说动词"说"的英译策略统计

策略 译本	对应		变换		显创		省略	
	数量	类别	数量	类别	数量	类别	数量	类别
蓝译本	17	1	10	1	54	48	22	1
%	16.5%		9.7%		52.4%		21.4%	
杨译本	42	1	12	3	44	35	7	1
%	40%		11.4%		42%		6.6%	

从以上表格可以看出,在4种策略中,杨译本使用对应和变换策略较多,分别为42例与12例,比蓝译本多出25例与2例;蓝译本则使用更多显创与省略的方法,分别使用54例(48类)与22例,比杨译本多出10例(13类)与15例。从数据上看,蓝译本言说动词的使用更加丰富多样。显创方法为言说动词使用丰富性的主要贡献者。

2. 感知动词

我们以最常见的感知动词"看见"为例,统计原文中的"看见"及两译本中see的使用频率。

表3.9 蓝译本与杨译本see和"看见"使用频率对比

项目	原文	蓝译本	杨译本
看见	128	0	0
see	0	363	486
合计	128	363	486

从上表可以看出,鲁迅小说《阿Q正传》原文有128例"看见",而两译本中,蓝译本使用典型视觉动词see(涵盖变体)363个,杨译本为486个,前者比后者少了123个。上表数据说明,两译本中,均有一定数量的see表达的并非"看见"的涵义;蓝译本与杨译本相比,蓝译本使用更少的see,因此,可能使用了更多其他动词表示"看见"。为了更加深入了解两译本具体使用了何种动词,运用了何种翻译策略,我们聚焦蓝译本与杨译本具体译例。总结下来,主要英译策略有以下几种:(1)对应,即see及其变体(sees, saw, seen, seeing);(2)变换,指其他表"看见"的表达,如名词sight,动词find等;(3)显创,即显化或创造,指译文根据语境对原文进行显化处理或为了修辞效果作"无中生有"的发挥创造,如使用spot等语义更为细致形象的下义词;(4)省略,即利用语境信息进行相应的省略处理。例句如下。

(1)对应

原文:阿Q看见自己的勋业得了赏识,便愈加兴高采烈起来:"和尚动得,我动不得?"他扭住伊的面颊。

杨译本：**Seeing** that his feat was admired, Ah Q began to feel elated. "If the monk paws you, why can't I?" Said he, pinching her cheek.

（2）变换

名词：

原文：他在路上走着要"求食"，看见熟识的酒店，看见熟识的馒头，但他都走过了，不但没有暂停，而且并不想要。

蓝译本：He walked past familiar **sights** — the tavern, trays of steamed rolls—without pausing, without registering a twinge of desire for either.

动词（词组）：

原文：这时他猛然间看见赵大爷向他奔来，而且手里捏着一支大竹杠。

蓝译本：He **became** swiftly **aware of** a rapid approach from Mr Zhao, who was holding a thick bamboo stick of his own.

介词：

原文：陈士成还看见许多小头夹着黑圆圈在眼前跳舞，有时杂乱，有时也摆成异样的阵图，然而渐渐的减少了，模胡了。

蓝译本：Seven heads and seven queues swayed **before** him, black circles dancing in the gaps between them.

（3）显创

原文：阿Q疑心他是和尚，但看见下面站着一排兵，两旁又站着十几个长衫人物……

蓝译本：Ah-Q wondered first if he was a monk, until he **spotted** rows of soldiers, together with some dozen important-looking individuals in long gowns…

（4）省略

原文：阿Q一看见，便赶紧翻身跟着逃。

蓝译本：Quick as he could, Ah-Q ran after him.

表 3.10 蓝译本与杨译本中感知动词"看见"的英译详细情况

策略	蓝译本	杨译本
对应	see（1/36）	see（1/70）
变换	became aware of; sight（7）; note（2）; sighting（2）; locate; before; find（3）; at the sight of; notice（4）; get…in sight（1）; glance（2）; look into; appear; catch sight of; in front of one's eye; be visible to; view…be blocked by; from（19/33）	sight（8）; catch sight of（2）; before; notice（4）; find（2）; meet; look at; look; appear; observe（10/22）
显创	come upon; spot（7）; stare（3）; conjure up; gaze at（2）; witness（2）; glance; be bereft of; pick out; swing into view; dawn; no way to make sb forget; swim into focus; sense; read; adjust to; catch…glimpse of; glimpse（动）; shine; make out（3）（20/32）	eyes fall on; glance at; interrupt; flash before; realize; read; catch a glimpse of; accustom to; dazzle by; make out; be witness to（11/11）
省略	omitted（1/26）	omitted（1/24）

表 3.11 蓝译本与杨译本感知动词"看见"英译策略统计

策略	对应		变换		显创		省略	
译本	数量	类别	数量	类别	数量	类别	数量	类别
蓝译本	36	1	33	19	32	20	26	1
%	28.3%		26%		25.1%		20%	
杨译本	70	1	22	10	11	11	24	1
%	55.1%		17.3%		8.6%		19%	

从以上表格可以看出，在4种策略中，杨译本对应策略使用较多，共为70例，蓝译本为36例，二者差距近1倍；两译本省略策略使用情况相当，蓝译本26例，杨译本24例，前者较后者多2例。再看变换与显创策略，蓝译本使用33例变换译法，32例显创译法，比重均高于杨译本。从数据上看，蓝译本对动词"看见"的翻译更加丰富多样。

本章小结

如前所述，动词是重要的词类，是叙事语言风格的重要指示牌，因此也是文学翻译风格的重点考察对象。本章基于语料库，对比了两类译本对实义动词的使用，得出以下结论：

（1）整体对比。从动词的形符、类符看，母语译者使用的动词类型均高于非母语译者，因此更为丰富；从平均词长来看，母语译者使用的动词均高于非母语译者，这反映了母语译者的用词正式度普遍高于非母语译者。这符合两类译者的总体词汇特征。

（2）翻译策略对比。我们进一步对比鲁迅小说的蓝译本与杨译本，聚焦两译本中对原文言说动词"说"以及感知动词"看见"的翻译，并总结了4种翻译策略：对应、变换、显创和省略。对比统计结果显示，在4种策略中，非母语译者杨宪益、戴乃迭偏向使用对应和变换策略；而母语译者译本蓝译本相对更多地使用显创策略。因此，蓝译本在言说动词和感知动词的表达上更加丰富多样。

第四章　名词使用对比

无论在何种语言中，名词都是非常重要的一种词性。而英汉两门语言相比，名词在英语中占据着更加重要的位置。因此，名词是探析汉译英小说词汇文体特征的重要指标。

一、总体名词对比

我们对 5 对译本的名词使用进行了统计，并重点关注 3 个指标，分别是词数、词类与平均词长。统计数据如下表所示。

表 4.1 母语—非母语译者译本名词使用统计表

原著	译本	形符	类符	平均词长
《浮生六记》	林译本	8177	2114	5.56
	拜伦译本	7985	1954	5.64
《聊斋志异》	大中华译本	10796	2209	5.49
	闵译本	11583	2643	5.73
《红楼梦》	杨译本	7845	2148	5.61
	霍译本	10314	2761	5.7
《骆驼祥子》	施译本	15722	3274	5.67
	葛译本	17029	3390	5.67
鲁迅小说	杨译本	17174	3395	5.7
	蓝译本	17314	3944	5.79

从名词数量与类别来看，5 对译本中，除了《浮生六记》，其他 4 对译本均以母语译者译本为高。单比词类，《红楼梦》的霍译本与杨译本差距最大，为 613 个；鲁迅小说蓝译本与杨译本差距次之，为 549 个；其后为《聊斋志异》的闵译本与大中华译本，两者相差 434 个；再者为《骆驼祥子》的葛译本与施译本，前者比后者

多出 116 个；而《浮生六记》的林译本与拜伦译本正好相反，作为非母语译者的林语堂，使用的名词类别反而比拜伦多出 160 个。比较各译本名词平均词长则发现，5 对译本中，母语译者译本该项数据均高于或等于非母语译者译本，其中《骆驼祥子》两译本平均词长相等。综合而言，母语译者的名词使用语体更偏正式。

我们再看各译本中不同长度名词的分布，如下表所示。

表 4.2 各译本不同长度名词的分布统计

原著	译本	3	4	5	6	7	8	9	10	>10
《浮生六记》	林译本	895	1924	1774	1454	891	534	349	193	163
	拜伦译本	703	1935	1742	1410	888	571	371	196	169
《聊斋志异》	大中华译本	1283	2591	2375	1885	1071	734	433	202	222
	闵译本	1350	2581	2096	2170	1255	842	593	333	363
《红楼梦》	杨译本	738	1916	1749	1295	874	598	338	152	185
	霍译本	1080	2500	2158	1509	1159	738	581	260	329
《骆驼祥子》	施译本	1591	3626	3403	2327	1814	1611	702	364	284
	葛译本	1848	4046	3492	2454	1795	1791	837	399	367
鲁迅小说	杨译本	1451	4392	3551	2818	1891	1218	990	437	426
	蓝译本	1601	4182	3403	2736	1948	1392	930	572	550

上表中的数据分布与各译本总体各长度词汇分布相符，即母语译者译本中，词长较长的名词频率相对较高。

二、抽象名词

与汉语相比，英语是相对抽象的语言，其抽象性主要表现在使用大量抽象名词，这类名词涵义概括，指称笼统，覆盖面广，往往有一种"虚、泛、暗、曲、隐"的魅力，因而便于用来表达复杂的思想和微妙的情绪。英语形成抽象表达的主要手段之一是用虚化词缀构词，前缀后缀皆有，后缀尤多。我们统计了由 5 种最常见抽象名词后缀构成的抽象名词。这 5 类后缀分别是：-ion、-ness、-ment、-ty 和 -ance/ence，均表达性质、状态之义。

表 4.3 各译本五类抽象名词统计

原著	译本	数量	类别
《浮生六记》	林译本	427	188
	拜伦译本	378	182
《聊斋志异》	大中华译本	504	210
	闵译本	624	294
《红楼梦》	杨译本	369	193
	霍译本	706	350
《骆驼祥子》	施译本	794	332
	葛译本	970	357
鲁迅小说	杨译本	910	323
	蓝译本	1185	461

从统计数据可以看出，除了《浮生六记》的林译本，其余 4 个译本中，非母语译者使用的抽象名词无论在数量上还是种类上，都低于母语译者。悬殊最大的为《红楼梦》的两个译本，霍译本使用的抽象名词比杨译本多出 337 个，并多出 157 种类，具有显著的差异。悬殊第二的为鲁迅小说的两个译本，蓝译本较杨译本的抽象名词多出 275 个，共计 138 种。悬殊最小的《浮生六记》的译本，林译本虽比拜伦译本多使用了 49 个抽象名词，但二者在种类上只差 6 种。

（一）鲁迅小说蓝译本与杨译本中 absence/presence 使用对比

如上表所示，总体而言，母语译者使用的抽象名词无论在数量上还是种类上都高于非母语译者。以鲁迅小说的蓝译本与杨译本为例。蓝译本共有抽象名词 461 种，1185 个，较杨译本的抽象名词多出 138 种，275 个。

那么，母语译者和非母语译者在抽象名词的运用上为何会出现此种系统性差异呢？我们以常见抽象名词 absence 和 presence 为例，考察鲁迅小说蓝译本与杨译本翻译策略的异同。蓝译本使用了 11 例 absence 和 6 例 presence，杨译本有 1 例 absence 和 2 例 presence。

1. Absence 使用对比

《牛津高阶英汉双解词典（第七版）》对 absence 常用释义有两项：① 缺席，

不在；② 不存在；缺乏。11 个译例大概分为以下 3 种情况。

（1）将形容词译为抽象名词

原文：他仔细一想，终于省悟过来：其原因盖在自己的<u>赤膊</u>。

蓝译本：Eventually, it dawned on him that the root cause of it all was the **absence** of his shirt.

杨译本：Careful thought led him to the conclusion that this was probably because his back **was bare**.

蓝译本中用 absence 来翻译"赤膊"中的形容词"赤"，以抽象名词对应形容词，而杨译本为直译，译为 be bare。

（2）将动词译为抽象名词

原文：……但他手里<u>没有</u>钢鞭，于是只得扑上去，伸手去拔小 D 的辫子。

蓝译本：Forced to improvise in the **absence** of a mace, he rushed forward to grab hold of D's queue.

杨译本：…but since he **had no** steel mace in his hand all he could do was to rush forward with outstretched hand to seize Young D's pigtail.

蓝译本将原文中的"没有"处理为抽象名词 absence，杨译本则做了直译。

原文：但夜深没有睡的既然只有两家，这单四嫂子家有声音，便自然只有老拱们听到，<u>没有</u>声音，也只有老拱们听到。

蓝译本：Since only two adjoining establishments stayed awake into the night, only Gong and his fellow drinkers would hear any noise that was to be heard from Mrs Shan's; or fail to hear it, in its **absence**.

杨译本：But since only two households were awake at midnight, Old Kung and the others were naturally the only ones who would notice if there were any sound from Fourth Shan's Wife's house, and the only ones to notice if **there were no** sound.

蓝译本将原文中的"没有"译为 absence，杨译本则调整为 there be 否定结构。

原文：我可是觉得在北京仿佛<u>没有</u>春和秋。

蓝译本：The **absence** of spring and autumn in Beijing — now that I noticed.

杨译本：It did seem to me though that Beijing **had no** spring or autumn.

原文中的"没有"被分别译为 absence 和 had no。

原文：到后半夜，还是毫无结果。

蓝译本：As the night edged towards dawn, there was still an **absence** of agreement.

杨译本：By the early hours of the morning they had reached **no** solution.

原文中的动词"无"在母语译者译本中转换为抽象名词，但非母语译者做了直译。

原文：阿Q忽然很羞愧自己没志气：竟没有唱几句戏。

蓝译本：Ah-Q was suddenly ashamed of his **absence** of spirit: of his failure even to croak out a few lines of opera.

杨译本：Ah Q suddenly became ashamed of his **lack** of spirit, because he had not sung any lines from an opera.

两译本中的动词"没"均译为抽象名词，前者为 absence，后者为 lack。

（3）将否定副词译为抽象名词

原文：所以大家主张继续罢课的时候，他虽然仍未到场，事后却尤其心悦诚服的确守了公共的决议。

蓝译本：…and when everyone else was in favour of going on with the strike, he wholeheartedly endorsed the decision (taken in his **absence**).

杨译本：…thus when everybody proposed remaining on strike although he still did **not attend** the meeting, he gladly abided later by the general decision.

原文中表示不在场的动词，蓝译本使用抽象名词做了意译，杨译本做了直译。

原文：子君不在我这破屋里时，我什么也看不见。

蓝译本：When Zijun was not here, I was blind to my decrepit surroundings, dazed by the unending tedium of her **absence**.

杨译本：In Tzu-chun's **absence**, I saw nothing in this shabby room.

两译本均使用了抽象名词 absence 来译原文中的动词。

原文：我冒了严寒，回到相隔二千余里，<u>别了</u>二十余年的故乡去。

蓝译本：After a twenty-year **absence**, and a journey of seven hundred bitterly cold miles, I returned home.

杨译本：Braving the bitter cold, I travelled more than seven hundred miles back to the old home I had **left** over twenty years before.

蓝译本将动词"别了"译为抽象名词 absence，而杨译本则译为对应的动词 leave。

原文：一个大教育家说道"教员一手挟书包一手要钱<u>不</u>高尚"，他才对于他的太太正式的发牢骚了。

蓝译本：It was on the day that one of the country's great educationalists attacked Fang's esteemed profession for their mercenary **absence** of dignity, for 'holding their lecture notes in one hand, and asking for money with the other, that he was at last roused to make a formal complaint to his wife.

杨译本：However, not until an outstanding educationist said, "It is **in poor taste** for teachers, a briefcase in one hand, to hold out the other for money," did he make any formal complaint to his wife.

原文"不高尚"中的否定副词"不"在蓝译本中被处理为抽象名词，而杨译本使用了一个介词短语"in poor taste"。

原文：孔乙己刚用指甲蘸了酒，想在柜上写字，见我毫<u>不</u>热心，便又叹一口气，显出极惋惜的样子。

蓝译本：Kong Yiji sighed—his fingernail already dipped in wine, ready to scrawl the characters across the bar—at my lamentable **absence** of academic zeal.

杨译本：Kung I-chi had dipped his finger in wine, in order to trace the characters on the counter; but when he saw how **indifferent** I was, he sighed and looked most disappointed.

蓝译本使用抽象名词，杨译本使用否定前缀 in-。

2. Presence 使用对比

Presence 的常用释义有 3 项：①（of a person 人）在场，出席；②（of a thing or substance）存在，出现；③ IDM：in the presence of sb/sth; in sb's presence 在……面前；有……在场。

（1）将动词译为抽象名词

原文：我想：希望本是无所谓<u>有</u>，无所谓无的。

蓝译本：Hope, I thought to myself, is an intangible **presence** that can neither be affirmed nor denied—a path that exists only where others have already passed.

杨译本：I thought: hope cannot be said to **exist**, nor can it be said not to exist.

原文中的动词"有"，蓝译本译为抽象名词 presence，杨译本使用了相应的动词 exit。

原文：按一按衣袋，硬硬的还<u>在</u>。

蓝译本：He patted his pocket again, to check for the robust **presence** of the silver.

杨译本：He patted his pocket—the hard packet **was** still **there**.

杨译本使用了 there be 结构来表达原文中的"在"。

原文：晚饭摆出来了，四叔俨然的<u>陪着</u>。

蓝译本：Uncle was a solemn **presence** through dinner.

杨译本：Dinner was served, and my uncle solemnly **accompanied** me.

杨译本将动词"陪着"译为 accompany。

（2）将形容词译为抽象名词

原文：我同时便机械的拧转身子，用力往外只一挤，觉得背后便已<u>满满的</u>……

蓝译本：I spun round and began shoving my way out of the crowd. The moment I retreated, I felt a **fleshy presence** pressing in behind me…

杨译本：Mechanically I turned round, and tried with might and main to shove my way out. I felt the place behind me **fill up** at once…

蓝译本将原文形容词"满满的"译为抽象名词,杨译本使用了动词短语"fill up"。

(3)将介词短语译为抽象名词

原文:她<u>在</u>大人<u>面前</u>还是这样。

蓝译本:See what I had to put up with?

杨译本:She dares act like this even in Seventh Master's **presence**.

杨译本将介词短语"在……面前"译为 presence,蓝译本利用语境予以省略。

原文:这把戏一个人玩不起来,必须<u>在</u>金龙<u>之前</u>,摆一个金鼎,注满清水,用兽炭煎熬。

蓝译本:But the performance requires more than its conjuror: it needs a golden cauldron filled with water, heated with charcoal and set before a king.

杨译本:I can't do this alone, though. It must be in the **presence** of a golden dragon, and I must have a golden cauldron filled with clear water and heated with charcoal.

同上,杨译本将介词短语"在……之前"译为 presence,蓝译本利用语境予以省略。

(4)其他情况

原文:赵太太还怕他因为春天的条件不敢来,而赵太爷以为不足虑:因为这是"我"去<u>叫</u>他的。

蓝译本:Mrs Zhao expressed concern that Ah-Q was too frightened to come, because of the events of last spring. Mr Zhao batted her worries away: this time, he had personally **commanded** Ah-Q's **presence**.

杨译本:Mrs. Chao was afraid that Ah Q dared not come because of the terms agreed upon that spring, but Mr. Chao did not think this anything to worry about, because, as he said, "This time I **sent for** him."

原文中动词"叫"间接表达"在场"之义,蓝译本使用了 command sb's presence,杨译本则使用了对应性更强的表达 send for sb。

原文：（嫦娥）慢慢回过头来，似理不理的向他看了一眼，没有答应。

蓝译本：Slowly turning around, she cursorily **acknowledged his presence with the briefest of glances**. She said nothing.

杨译本：She turned slowly and **threw him an indifferent glance** without returning his greeting.

原文中的"向……看了一眼"在蓝译本中被处理为 acknowledge sb's presence，而同样，杨译本则将其译为语义结构较为对应的表达：throw sb a glance。

对比以上数据与案例，我们不难得出初步结论：①母语译者偏好使用抽象名词；②母语译者使用抽象名词所涉及的情景丰富多样，原文的名词、动词、形容词、副词等皆可演绎成为抽象名词表达，策略灵活多样。相比之下，非母语译者使用抽象名词数量少，场景单一，只有两种情景下使用了抽象名词，一例中"不在"被译为 absence，另两例中将"在……之（面）前"译为 presence，语义对应性较强，策略欠灵活。

（二）鲁迅小说蓝译本与杨译本 -ity 后缀抽象名词使用对比

为了验证上面的初步结论，我们对鲁迅小说蓝译本与杨译本进行更广泛的抽样调查。我们提取了蓝译本与杨译本中 -ity 后缀的独特抽象名词。相对于杨译本，蓝译本共使用 36 种后缀为 -ity 的独特抽象名词，共计 46 例；相对于蓝译本，杨译本共有 13 种蓝译本中未出现的后缀为 -ity 的抽象名词，共 19 例。从这一对比来看，蓝译本的抽象名词使用更加丰富多样。具体对比数据如下。

表 4.4 -ity 后缀抽象名词使用对比

蓝译本独特 -ity 结尾单词	杨译本独特 -ity 结尾单词
类符数：36 形符数：46	类符数：13 形符数：19

（续表）

蓝译本独特 -ity 结尾单词	杨译本独特 -ity 结尾单词
authority 1，celebrity 4，clarity 2，dignity 4，eccentricity 1，hostility 1，humanity 2，reality 2，similarity 1，absurdity 1，animosity 1，capacity 1，cordiality 1，desirability 1，duality 1，enormity 1，falsity 1，fecundity 1，ferocity 1，inability 1，indemnity 1，indispensability 1，insecurity 1，maturity 1，immortality 2，obscurity 1，personality 1，quality 1，sanctity 1，scarcity 1，sincerity 1，solemnity 1，superiority 1，temerity 1，vulgarity 1，vulnerability 1	enmity 3，integrity 3，nobility 3，calamity 1，illogicality 1，incapacity 1，liability 1，originality 1，seniority 1，severity 1，simplicity 1，tranquility 1，vitality 1

我们将 -ity 后缀抽象名词所涉及的翻译策略总结为 3 类：对应型、改换型与显创型。1. 对应型抽象，即以抽象名词译抽象名词，如将"和气"译为 cordiality；2. 改换型抽象，指将具象名词或动词、形容词等其他词性的词语译为抽象名词，如将具象名词"身子"译为 mortality，将动词"明白"译为 clarity，将形容词"可笑的"译为 absurdity；3. 显创型抽象，即显化或创造，指译文根据语境对原文进行显化处理或为了修辞效果作"无中生有"的发挥创造，译出抽象名词。

具体例句如下：

1. 对应型抽象

原文：大家的腰骨都似乎直得多，原先收紧着的脸相也宽懈下来，全客厅顿然见得一团<u>和气</u>了。

蓝译本：Everyone straightened up, and the tension on the assembled company's faces relaxed into expressions of relieved **cordiality**.

杨译本：They all seemed to draw themselves up, and their tense expressions relaxed. Complete **harmony** prevailed.

原文：我没有负着<u>虚伪</u>的重担的勇气，却将真实的重担卸给她了。

蓝译本：Lacking the courage to bear the burden of **falsity**, I set upon her the heavier burden of the truth.

杨译本：I hadn't the courage to shoulder the heavy burden of **hypocrisy**, so I thrust the burden of the truth on to her.

2. 改换型抽象

原文：他对着浮游在碧海里似的月亮，觉得自己的<u>身子</u>非常沉重。

蓝译本：Gazing upon it now, floating in a sea of deep blue, he felt the heaviness of his own **mortality**.

杨译本：As he watched the moon floating in a sapphire sea, his own **limbs** seemed very heavy.

原文：凡事须得研究，才会<u>明白</u>。

蓝译本：Only thorough investigation will bring **clarity**.

杨译本：Everything requires careful consideration if one is to **understand** it.

原文：他在不妥帖的衣冠中，安静地躺着，合了眼，闭着嘴，口角间仿佛含着冰冷的微笑，冷笑着这<u>可笑的死尸</u>。

蓝译本：There he lay, under all this improbable clothing, eyes and mouth shut, lips curled up at the corners, mocking his posthumous **absurdity**.

杨译本：In his awkward costume he lay placidly, with closed mouth and eyes. There seemed to be an ironical smile on his lips, mocking the **ridiculous** corpse.

3. 显创型抽象

原文：阿 Q 自然都答应了，可惜没有钱。

蓝译本：Regrettably, Ah-Q lacked the funds to make good his **indemnity**.

杨译本：Ah Q naturally agreed to everything, but unfortunately he had no ready money.

原文：这一场"龙虎斗"似乎并无胜败，也不知道看的人可满足……

蓝译本：There was a certain **lack of clarity and closure** about this particular battle between the dragon and tiger of Weizhuang. Who was victor? Who was vanquished? Was the audience satisfied with the performance?

杨译本：This epic struggle had **apparently ended neither in victory nor defeat**, and it is not known whether the spectators were satisfied or not…

根据上述分类，我们对鲁迅小说蓝译本与杨译本中 -ity 抽象名词所涉及的翻译策略相关数据统计如下。

表 4.5 蓝译本与杨译本独特 –ity 抽象名词翻译策略统计

策略		对应	变换	显创
蓝译本	数量	9	28	10
	%	19%	60%	21%
杨译本	数量	8	9	1
	%	44.4%	50%	5.6%

蓝译本采用对应策略的译例为 9 例, 占比为 19%, 杨译本中该策略译例有 8 例, 占比 44%, 显著高于蓝译本。蓝译本中变换策略为 28 例, 占比为 60%, 为抽象名词所涉及的主要翻译策略；杨译本中该策略为 9 例, 占比 50%, 略低于蓝译本, 亦是主要策略。就显创策略而言, 蓝译本 10 例, 占比 21%, 而杨译本仅 1 例, 占比 5.6%, 显著低于蓝译本。从以上数据可以看出, 蓝译本中变换策略与显创策略合计占比 81%, 杨译本中该比例为 55.6%, 相比之下, 蓝译本抽象名词的使用更为灵活。

三、名词复现

词汇复现是词汇衔接中的一个重要方面。英汉在词汇衔接上表现出系统的差异。除非有意强调或出于修辞的需要, 英语总的倾向是尽量避免重复 (连淑能 2010)。这在很大程度上是因为"英语的同义词和近义词极为丰富, 数量也比汉语多, 因而也便于通过同义词、近义词替换来变换表达方式" (连淑能 2010)。这就不难理解, 英语中里同形回指现象很少 (强调和修辞除外) (蒋和舟 2007)。而与英语相反, 重复是汉语的一个明显特点 (陈定安 1998), 即使用同形回指的频率大大高于英语语篇。有学者指出, 中文语篇中词汇的简单重复十分普遍, 尤其是名词、称呼语的重复 (徐剑英 2005)。异形回指, 接近修辞上的 elegant variation (有译为"换词求雅"), 即使用非代词性替代表达回指上文出现过的表达 (Leech & Short 2001)。英汉两种语言在回指使用上的差异不仅体现在母语语篇创作上, 也体现在译文中。不同译者, 尤其是译入语为母语的译者和译出语为母语的译者在译文创作中对篇章回指的使用常常表现出不同的特征。此处, 我们聚焦鲁迅小说的蓝译本与杨译本针对"秀才"与"举人"两个名词所采用的翻译策略,以揭示母语译者与非母语译者之间的风格差异。

(一)"秀才"英译对比

原文中关于秀才的表达有两类:一指秀才的身份或资质,或指这一类人,一般出现在"隽秀才""进秀才""变秀才""捞秀才"等动词短语中,此种表达有6例;二指秀才其人,有26例。

针对6例第一类"秀才",蓝译本、杨译本具体译文如下。

表4.6 "秀才"相关动词短语翻译对比

No.	原文	蓝译本	杨译本
1	进秀才	romp through the lowest, county-level stage of the civil service examination	pass the county examination
2	变秀才	get through at least the lowest rung of the official examinations	pass the official examinations
3	隽秀才①	pass the county-level civil service examination	pass the official examination
4	隽秀才②	with the county competition behind him	win one's first degree in the country examination
5	捞秀才	pass an exam	pass the lowest official examination
6	未进秀才时候	revise for evening	before Mr. Chao's son passed the county examination

针对第二类"秀才",蓝译本与杨译本具体译例如下。

表4.7 "秀才"相关名词翻译对比

No.	蓝译本	杨译本
秀才	local genius(2); village genius(11); young gentleman of letters(1); the man of letters(1); his son(2); his learned son(2); the Zhao son(1); younger Zhao(1); his(1); the latter(1);省略(3)	successful candidate(7); successful county candidate(17); his(1); scholars who…(1)
	11/26	4/26

从表达方式来看，蓝译本有 4 类表达方式：① 动词 + through examination；② pass examination；③ with examination behind；④ revise。相比之下，杨译本用了 2 类表达方式：① pass examination；② win degree in examination。我们进一步审视可发现，蓝译本先后使用了 lowest, county-level stage，lowest rung 以及 county-level，表达秀才所对应的科举考试级别，而杨译本的处理则相对单一。蓝译本另使用 examination 与 competition 两个单词表示考试，杨译本仅使用前者。

针对后 26 例"秀才"的翻译，蓝译本共使用 6 类 11 种表达：（1）local/village genius（13 例）；（2）man/gentleman of letters（2 例）；（3）one's/Zhao son（6 例）；（4）his（1 例）；（5）the latter（1 例）；（6）省略（3 例）。杨译本使用了 3 类 4 种表达：（1）successful（county）candidate（24 例）；（2）his（1 例）；（3）scholars who have passed the examination（1 例）。不难看出，蓝译本的翻译方式灵活多变一些。

（二）"举人"英译对比

再看"举人"。原文共两种表达，一为举人；二为举人老爷。译文汇总如下。

表 4.8　"举人"翻译对比

No	蓝译本	杨译本
举人	a local bigwig who had passed the provincial- level civil service examination（1）；provincial examination laureate（1）；Mr. Provincial Examination（12）；the revered gentleman（1）；the great scholar（1）；the great man of learning（1）；the esteemed man of letters（1）；the discomforted scholar（1）；the former（1）；Mr. Ding, the magistrate（1）；省略（3）	scholars who have passed them（1）；the successful provincial candidate（19）；successful candidate（1）；such a man（1）；the scholar（1）；Mr. Ting，the provincial scholar（1）
	11/24	6/24

针对 24 例"举人"的翻译，蓝译本共使用 11 种表达，杨译本使用了 6 种表达。同样，蓝译本的翻译策略更加灵活，手段更加多样，译文更加符合英语的词汇复现特征。

本章小结

本章对比母语译者与非母语译者的名词使用特征，得出以下结论。

① 总体特征。我们通过比较各译本名词平均词长后发现，总体而言，母语译者译本名词平均长度高于非母语译者译本名词平均长度，由此可知，母语译者译本名词的语体更加正式。值得注意的是，《浮生六记》的林译本名词平均词长高于拜伦译本，从侧面印证林译本的独特特征。两类译本的名词语域特征与其总体特征对比相契合。

② 抽象名词使用对比。我们通过对比 5 种最常见抽象名词后缀构成的抽象名词后发现，母语译者译本使用的抽象名词无论在数量上还是种类上均高于非母语译者译本。同样，《浮生六记》的林译本仍是非典型的非母语译者译本。我们通过进一步细致比较鲁迅小说蓝译本与杨译本中的抽象名词后发现，母语译者使用抽象名词所涉及的情景丰富多样，原文的名词、动词、形容词、副词等皆可演绎成为抽象名词表达，策略灵活多样。如果将翻译策略划分为对应型、变换型、显创型 3 类，则蓝译本中后两类策略占比达 81%，远高于非母语译者的 55.6%。这说明蓝译本较杨译本策略更为灵活。

③ 名词复现对比。我们通过对比鲁迅小说的蓝译本与杨译本针对"秀才"与"举人"两个名词所采用的翻译策略后发现，在翻译这两个高频名词时，蓝译本各使用 11 种表达，杨译本仅使用 4 种和 6 种表达，相比之下，蓝译本词汇使用更加丰富。

第五章　形容词使用对比

形容词是几大主要词性之一，主要用来描写或修饰名词或代词，表示人或事物的性质、状态、特征或属性。其在数量和种类上所呈现出的差异，是衡量译者风格的重要指标之一，值得深入研究。

形容词可作若干分类。有学者（薄冰，2000）将形容词根据其与所修饰的名词的关系，分为限制性形容词（restrictive adjective）与描写性形容词（descriptive adjective）。其中，限制性形容词表示事物的本质，与被修饰词关系紧密，可视为一体，一旦缺席，影响名词的意义，如 a Catholic church；描写性形容词又称为非限制性形容词，作进一步描述之用，即便省去，不影响被修饰词的本义，如 an impressive Catholic church。也有更加精细的划分。辛克莱（2007）根据功用列举了若干种形容词。有定性形容词（qualitative adjective），用来说明某人或某物具有某种特性，如 sad, pretty, happy, wise 等；有分类形容词（classifying adjective），用于说明某物的类型，比 **financial** help, **daily** shower, **Victorian** houses, **civil** engineering；有颜色形容词（colour adjective），用以说明某物的颜色；有强调形容词（emphasizing adjective），强调对某物所作的描述或某物的程度，如 He made me look like a complete fool; Some of it was absolute rubbish；有说明形容词（specifying adjective），置于限定词之后和其他形容词之前，用来准确说明提及的内容，如 He wore his **usual** old white coat.。另有一些学习资源对形容词做了相当细致的分类：（1）专有形容词（proper adjectives），如 the **English** language；（2）描写性形容词（descriptive adjective），如 the **brave** solider；（3）量形容词（quantitative adjective），如 **much** bread；（4）数形容词（numeral adjective），如 **six** monkeys；（5）指示形容词（demonstrative adjective），如 give me **that** book；

（6）分配形容词（distributive adjective），如 **each** solider；（7）疑问形容词（interrogative adjectives），如 **what** language；（8）所有格形容词（possessive adjective），如 **their** luggage。

根据本研究的目的，并考虑到数据统计与分析的可行性，我们重点关注以下两类形容词：一是强调形容词；二是定性形容词或描写性形容词。此外，我们还关注两类译本中形容词的最高级表达。

一、形容词使用总体特征

我们先对5对译本的形容词进行统计，数据如下表所示。

表 5.1 母语—非母语译者形容词数据对比

译本	形符	类符
母语译者译本	21794	2887
非母语译者译本	23708	2506
相差	−1914	381

整体来看，母语译者所使用形容词的绝对数量比非母语译者少，二者累计相差1914；但从种类上来看，母语译者多出381，这意味着母语译者形容词使用虽然频率稍低，但类别更加丰富。这一数据符合母语译者与非母语译者的整体词汇对比情况。下面为5对译本的具体数据对比。

表 5.2 母语—非母语译者形容词数据对比

译本	鲁迅小说		《聊斋志异》		《红楼梦》		《骆驼祥子》		《浮生六记》	
	杨译本	蓝译本	大中华译本	闵译本	杨译本	霍译本	施译本	葛译本	林译本	拜伦译本
类符	1276	1485	782	1004	720	1073	1295	1351	755	634
形符	6230	6042	3198	3884	2483	3600	5974	5950	2625	2358

从形容词数量来看，《聊斋志异》的闵译本与《红楼梦》的霍译本这两个母语译者译本多于大中华译本与杨译本，其他3部作品的母语译者译本均低于非母语

译者译本。从类别来看，除了《浮生六记》，其他4对译本中，母语译者译本均高于非母语译者译本。值得注意的是，《浮生六记》的林译本所使用的形容词在数量和类别上均高于母语译者译本。

二、强调性形容词

我们使用语料库工具统计母语译者与非母语译者的关键形容词，两类译本中各取排名前十的关键形容词，数据如下。

表5.3 母语—非母语译者关键形容词对比

非母语译者 删节前类符数：2506 删节后类符数：1450			母语译者 删节前类符数：2887 删节后类符数：2215		
No.	keyword	frequency	keyness	keyword	frequency	keyness
1	successful	50	56.823	own	430	24.446
2	whole	253	43.804	-th	26	22.9
3	imperial	54	43.526	local	58	19.969
4	tamer	28	36.509	occasional	24	17.583
5	big	194	23.888	proper	44	17.438
6	old	899	21.984	aware	45	15.581
7	several	208	20.502	great	241	15.554
8	-stricken	12	15.647	tiny	48	15.537
9	good	463	14.985	little	406	14.969
10	high	124	14.098	filthy	19	14.359

从以上数据可以看出，母语译者译本中关键值排名第一的为强调性形容词own。我们接下来将深入细致地探讨母语译者译本与非母语译者译本中强调性形容词的使用差异。

(一)强调性形容词 own 使用对比

该词在 5 对译本中使用分布情况如下表所示。

表 5.4 强调性形容词 own 在 5 对译本中使用分布情况

关键词	译本	鲁迅小说	《聊斋志异》	《红楼梦》	《骆驼祥子》	《浮生六记》
own	非母语译者译本	63	25	41	137	27
	母语译者译本	113	106	100	97	14
	相差	50	81	59	-40	-13

形容词 own 意思为"自己的,本人的",表强调。该词在鲁迅小说、《聊斋志异》和《红楼梦》母语译者译本中的使用频率分别为 113 次、106 次、100 次,均远远高于其所对应的非母语译者译本;在《红楼梦》和《骆驼祥子》中,非母语译者使用频率较高,但差距幅度不如前三对译本。整体看来,own 是母语译者译本中的关键形容词。我们以《阿 Q 正传》为例,看看两译本对 own 一词的使用差异。译本中 own 有如下 3 种使用情况。

1. 对应

所谓对应,即原文也使用了"自己(的)""亲(自)""本"等强调表达,译文做了对应的处理。

原文:"你到外面来……不要躲在<u>自己</u>房里想……"

蓝译本:"Come on out." Mr Zhao's daughter-in-law was trying to coax Mrs Wu out of the servants' quarters. "Don't let it upset you."

杨译本:"Come outside… don't stay brooding in your **own** room."

原文:小 D 一手护住了自己的辫根,一手也来拔阿 Q 的辫子,阿 Q 便也将空着的一只手护住了<u>自己</u>的辫根。

蓝译本:His opponent left one hand protecting the base of the pigtail, while attacking Ah-Q's **own** queue with his other.

杨译本:Young D, while protecting his pigtail with one hand, tried to seize Ah Q's

第五章　形容词使用对比

with the other, whereupon Ah Q also used one free hand to protect his **own** pigtail.

原文：吃完之后，又要了一支点过的四两烛和一个树烛台，点起来，独自躺在<u>自己的</u>小屋里。

蓝译本：Ah-Q ate them and asked for a candlestick and four-ounce candle, which he lit, then lay down alone in his **own** small room.

杨译本：Ah Q asked him for two flat cakes, and after eating these demanded a four-ounce candle that had been used, and a candlestick. He lit the candle and lay down alone in his little room.

原文：他关好大门，摸进<u>自己的</u>屋子里。

蓝译本：Locking the main gate, he groped his way to his **own** room though an absolute darkness.

杨译本：When he had closed the big gate he groped his way into his room.

原文：阿Q又很<u>自</u>尊，所有未庄的居民，全不在他眼神里……

蓝译本：Ah-Q had a robust sense of his **own** self-worth, placing the rest or Weizhuang far beneath him in the social scale.

杨译本：Ah Q, again, had a very high opinion of himself. He looked down on all the inhabitants of Weichuang…

原文：阿Q的耳朵里，本来早听到过革命党这一句话，今年又<u>亲</u>眼见过杀掉革命党。

蓝译本：Revolutionaries were old news to Ah-Q: why, earlier that year, he had watched them being executed.

杨译本：Ah Q had long since known of revolutionaries, and this year with his **own** eyes had seen revolutionaries being decapitated.

原文：况且做这路生意的大概是"老鹰不吃窝下食"：本村倒不必担心的……

蓝译本：As likely as not, someone in his line of business wouldn't shit on his own doorstep. The villagers had nothing to worry about…

杨译本：...in a business like this it was probably a case of "the eagle does not prey on its own nest": his **own** village need not worry...

2. 增强

译文中出现 own 的第二种情况为增强，即原文提供了隐含的语境线索，译文对该语用涵义做了强化，如将原文的"他的"译成 his own。

原文：这虽然也在他身上，而看阿Q的意思，倒也似乎以为不足贵的……

蓝译本：Although they were of his **own** revered body's making, Ah-Q felt them unworthy of him...

杨译本：Although these were on his **own** head, apparently Ah Q did not consider them as altogether honourable...

原文：谁料这小子竟谋了他的饭碗去。

蓝译本：Never, in his worst nightmares, would Ah-Q have dreamt that this utter weed would make off with his **own** bowl of rice.

杨译本：Who could have thought that this low fellow would steal his living from him?

原文："锵锵，"阿Q料不到他的名字会和"老"字联结起来。

蓝译本："Clang clang-clang," he sang on, too nonplussed by the word "friend" to connect it with his **own** name, supposing he had misheard.

杨译本："Tra la!" sang Ah Q, unable to imagine that his name could be linked with those words "old chap".

原文：抬得他自己有些不信他的眼睛了。

蓝译本：Incredulous, and yet resolved to go no closer, he returned to the temple.

杨译本：...carrying until he could hardly believe his **own** eyes.

3. 创造

第三种情况为创造，即译者做了意译，与原文并无必然的逻辑对应，属于再创造。

第五章　形容词使用对比

原文：而终于归接到传阿Q，仿佛思想里有鬼似的。

蓝译本：Contrast my **own** humble fixation – like that of a man possessed – on recording the life of Ah-Q, otherwise.

杨译本：But in the end, as though possessed by some fiend, I always came back to the idea of writing the story of Ah Q.

原文：因为从来不朽之笔，须传不朽之人，于是人以文传，文以人传……

蓝译本：A biographer hungry for glory must find his **own** genius mirrored by the genius of his subject…

杨译本：…for an immortal pen has always been required to record the deeds of an immortal man…

原文：此后每逢揪住他黄辫子的时候，人就先一着对他说……

蓝译本：Ah-Q's tormentors learned of his habit of declaring moral victory over the ashes of defeat, and added their **own** revisions while yanking on his queue…

杨译本：So after this anyone who pulled or twisted his brown pigtail would forestall him by saying…

原文：然而不到十秒钟，阿Q也心满意足的得胜的走了……

蓝译本：And yet within ten seconds, Ah-Q had set jubilantly off on his **own** way…

杨译本：In less than ten seconds, however, Ah Q would walk away also satisfied that he had won…

原文：赵秀才消息灵，一知道革命党已在夜间进城……

蓝译本：The moment the village genius heard, through his **own** channels of communication, that the Revolutionary Party had taken the town during the night…

杨译本：The successful county candidate in the Chao family learned the news quickly, and as soon as he heard that the revolutionaries had entered the town that night…

原文：洋先生却没有见他，因为白着眼睛讲得正起劲……

蓝译本：Mr Foreigner was too busy with his **own** impassioned speech, however, to have eyes for Ah-Q…

杨译本：But Mr. Foreigner had not seen him, because with eyes raised he was saying with great animation…

原文：他便知道这人一定有些来历，膝关节立刻自然而然的宽松，便跪了下去了。

蓝译本：At this point, he realized this was an encounter with Authority; his joints automatically weakened and reduced him to his knees.

杨译本：…he knew this man must be someone important. At once the joints of his knees relaxed **of their own accord**, and he sank down.

我们对上述译例做简单的统计，发现蓝译本共使用 own 一词 12 次，其中对应 3 次，增强 3 次，创造 6 次；相比之下，杨译本使用 6 次，仅为蓝译本数量的一半，其中对应 3 次，与蓝译本一致，增强 2 次，创造仅 1 次，并且属于固定搭配。从数量与翻译方法上来看，蓝译本更倾向于使用 own 来强调，翻译策略也更加灵活。

（二）其他强调性形容词使用对比

我们由上想到，蓝译本对于强调性形容词 own 的偏好究竟是个案，还是母语译者的某种统一选择呢？我们统计对比了 5 对译本中 5 个常见强调性形容词的使用情况。

表 5.5 常见强调性形容词对比统计

译本 单词	鲁迅小说		《红楼梦》		《聊斋志异》		《浮生六记》		《骆驼祥子》	
	蓝译本	杨译本	霍译本	杨译本	闵译本	大中华译本	拜伦译本	林译本	葛译本	施译本
only	37	21	10	8	17	12	12	9	45	27
single	14	14	4	5	19	2	3	5	9	11
very	9	3	5	3	27	7	3	3	2	3
particular	7	2	4	0	2	0	1	0	2	1
mere	2	2	2	1	0	1	1	2	3	3
合计	69	42	25	17	65	22	20	19	61	45

上表数据显示，就这 5 个强调性形容词而言，母语译者使用频率均高于非母语译者，印证了母语译者更倾向于使用强调性形容词。我们将在本书后面的章节中统计另一种强调性词汇手段——反身代词的使用情况。

三、形容词情感色彩对比

近义词虽然意义相近，但褒贬之义有区别，情感色彩有差异。形容词也不例外。近年来，随着语料库语言学的快速发展，二语习得领域学者特别关注词汇在搭配中所呈现出的语义倾向，即语义韵。语义韵的概念最早由 Sinclair(1991)提出，指的语义倾向受其搭配词的语义倾向影响所呈现在整个语境内的语义氛围。一般而言，语义韵有积极语义韵、消极语义韵和中性语义韵 3 种。在本研究中，我们主要关注单词的两种状态：①有较为强烈的情感意义；②情感意义较弱，趋于中性。

我们以表达"大"和"小"的近义形容词为例，窥探母语译者与非母语译者在形容词使用上是否有不同的选择倾向。我们统计了表示"大"的 3 个单词 big，large，great，以及表示"小"的三个单词 small，tiny，little。

我们分别对这两组近义形容词的情感色彩进行辨析。

Big 和 large 通常指具体事物的大小，big 多指程度、范围、规模，形容人时指人的身材高大；large 不如 big 常用，一般指体积、面积、容积、数量之大；great 带有感情色彩，有"巨大的、伟大的"之意。由此可见，与 big 和 large 相比，great 有较为强烈的情感意义。

Small 常用于指外形、尺寸等较小，属于中性；tiny 表示特别小，极小的，微小的，情感色彩较 small 强。little 是带有感情色彩的"小"，表示喜欢、可怜或讨厌等。Small，tiny，little 的情感色彩由弱到强。

我们统计对比了这两组 6 个单词在 5 对译本中的使用情况，如下表所示。

表 5.6 各译本表大小形容词使用对比

形容词	《聊斋志异》		《红楼梦》		鲁迅小说		《骆驼祥子》		《浮生六记》	
	大中华译本	闵译本	杨译本	霍译本	杨译本	蓝译本	施译本	葛译本	林译本	拜伦译本
big	<u>41</u>	7	12	<u>21</u>	<u>60</u>	28	<u>39</u>	31	<u>25</u>	19
large	8	<u>30</u>	6	<u>11</u>	<u>30</u>	23	<u>38</u>	32	0	<u>16</u>
great	20	<u>89</u>	14	<u>31</u>	82	<u>84</u>	35	<u>38</u>	29	29
small	<u>29</u>	18	<u>15</u>	3	<u>92</u>	50	<u>65</u>	36	35	<u>80</u>
tiny	4	<u>14</u>	1	<u>5</u>	4	<u>16</u>	4	<u>11</u>	<u>2</u>	1
little	37	<u>79</u>	32	<u>151</u>	<u>74</u>	64	<u>85</u>	78	<u>64</u>	30

big 的数量：除了《红楼梦》的霍译本外，其他均为非母语译者译本多于母语译者译本，其中，《聊斋志异》译本差距最大，大中华译本比闵译本多使用 34 个 big。

large 的数量：《聊斋志异》的闵译本、《红楼梦》的霍译本以及《浮生六记》的拜伦译本多于其对应的非母语译者译本，其中，《聊斋志异》译本悬殊最大，二者相差 22 个。

great 的数量：除了《浮生六记》两译本数量相同，其他 4 对译本中，母语译者译本均多于非母语译者译本，其中，《聊斋志异》译本差距最大，闵译本比大中华译本多使用 69 个 great。

small 的数量：除了《浮生六记》林译本，其他 4 对译本中，非母语译者译本均多于母语译者译本，其中，鲁迅小说译本差距最大，蓝译本比杨译本多使用 42 个 small。

tiny 的数量：除了《浮生六记》林译本，其他 4 对译本中，母语译者译本均多于非母语译者译本，其中，鲁迅小说译本差距最大，蓝译本比杨译本多使用 12 个 tiny。

little 的数量：5 对译本中，《聊斋志异》和《红楼梦》的母语译者译本较非母语译者译本使用更多的 little，并且悬殊较大，闵译本比大中华译本多 42 个，霍译本比杨译本多出 119 个。对比鲁迅小说和《骆驼祥子》的两对译本可发现非母语译者译本使用数量虽然多于母语译者译本，但差距较小，分别为 10 个和 7 个。值得注意的是，《浮生六记》的林译本比母语译者译本多34个，差距较为悬殊。

总体而言，母语译者译本比非母语译者译本更多使用情感色彩更加浓厚的形容词，二者数据统计如下表。

表5.7 母语——非母语译者表大小形容词使用汇总

形容词	母语译者	非母语译者	备注
big	106	177	-71
large	82	112	-30
great	271	180	91
small	187	236	-49
tiny	47	15	32
little	402	292	110

下面我们以《聊斋志异》中的great为例，更为细致地分析该词在母语译者译本与非母语译者译本中用法的差异。great在译本中大致有两种意义，一为表达规模之大和程度之甚；二为伟大。其大致对应3种翻译方法：对等，增显与创饰。

1. 对等

对等指将原文中有表达程度之甚的词语译为great。

原文：家君仰慕鸿才，常欲附为婚姻。

闵译本：My father admires your **great** accomplishments, and has long wanted to see you marry into our family.

大中华译本：My father, highly respectful of your accomplishments, has long wished to be your in-law.

原文中，"鸿才"中之"鸿"字表示程度，在闵译本中译为"great"，在大中华译本中做了简化处理。类似译例还有若干。

原文：与娇娜相伯仲也。生大悦……

闵译本：Kong observed to his **great** joy that she was every bit as beautiful as grace…

大中华译本：In beauty, she was in no way inferior to Jiaona. **Delighted**, Xueli asked the young master to be the go-between.

原文：慕君高雅……

闵译本：I have heard of you as a gentleman of **great** erudition and refinement…

大中华译本：I admire your grace and refined tastes very much.

原文：问妹子则嫁；岳母已亡：深相感悼。

闵译本：Kong also learned to his **great** sorrow that Pine's mother, his mother-in-law, had died.

大中华译本：Xueli inquired after Sister Jiaona and was told that she had married and her mother-in-law had passed away.

原文：辱膺宠命，何敢多辞？

闵译本：How could I ever presume to decline such a **great** honour…

大中华译本：Since you deign to grant me your **most** partial appointment, how dare I stubbornly decline?

原文：从梁间锵锵而下，势如骤雨。

闵译本：…thousands of coins came clattering down from the ceiling in a **great** shower…

大中华译本：…millions of coins began to fall like a downpour…making jingling sounds as they fell to the floor.

原文：设筵相款，宠礼异常。

闵译本：…served him a veritable banquet and treated him with **great** respect and affection…

大中华译本：…prepared a big meal for him, showering him with hospitality.

原文：众骇异，不解其故。

闵译本：We were both thrown into a **great** state of alarm…

大中华译本：Everyone was shocked and amazed…

以上这些译例的原文中，"大悦""高雅""深相""宠命""骤雨""宠礼异常""骇异"等词语本身均含有表程度的表达，闵译本皆使用 great 做对等处理，而大中华译本多数情况下均予以省略。

2. 增显

增显指原文中并无字面上表达程度之词，但其语用内涵有所暗示，因而译文也以 great 予以增强或明示。

原文：……翁脑裂不能言，俄顷已绝。

闵译本：...to find Old Bian...bleeding profusely from a **great gash** on his head.

大中华译本：...found her father fatally wounded. A moment later he died.

原文中"脑裂"一词，对程度的表达是隐性的，闵译本均使用了 great，同样，大中华译本以简化为主。类似的译例如下。

原文：河水倾泼丈余……

闵译本：...while **great** ten-foot **waves** came surging down the course of the river.

大中华译本：The water in the river was flung over ten feet high.

原文：栖霞山裂，沂水陷穴，广数亩。

闵译本：...the River Yi near the town of Yishui flowed into a **great depression** to form a lake of several acres.

大中华译本：Yi river had disappeared into a crater an acre across.

原文：痛楚呻吟。

闵译本：It gave him **great** pain and caused him to groan constantly.

大中华译本：He moaned and groaned incessantly as the pain was unbearable.

原文：中心懊丧，进退莫决。

闵译本：He was left in a state of **great distress**, quite at a loss what to do next.

大中华译本：The man was **very frustrated** and did not know how to handle this "male concubine".

3. 创饰

创饰指为了修辞效果所作的添加。

原文：孔生雪笠，<u>圣裔</u>也。

闵译本：Kong Xueli, a descendant of the **great sage** Confucius…

闵译本中的 great 与 big 相比有较强的情感，表示"伟岸、高大、惊人"之意，因此常被用作表赞叹、惊叹的修辞。类似的译例如下。

原文：力与蟒争，竟曳兄出。

闵译本：…he wrestled fiercely with the **great** snake…

大中华译本：After a tug-of-war with the **boa**…

原文：生如其教，果见娇娜偕<u>丽人</u>来……

闵译本：And watched Grace walking in the garden in the company of another young lady of **great beauty**…

大中华译本：He saw Jiaona coming, accompanying a pretty girl…

对如上问题，我们可以换一个视角。因这两组词可能对应的原文为"大"和"小"，我们将 3 对两组 6 个词与"大"和"小"分别在平行语料库中做共现检索，看看结果有何启示。其中，《聊斋志异》《红楼梦》以及鲁迅小说三对译本数据如下。

表 5.8 3 对译本母语—非母语译者和原文表大小形容词共现统计

形容词		《聊斋志异》			《红楼梦》			鲁迅小说		
		原文	大中华译本	闵译本	原文	杨译本	霍译本	原文	杨译本	蓝译本
大	big	28	21	10	21	14	13	73	53	21
	large	12	2	8	8	5	5	59	34	23
	great	22	8	18	16	9	9	100	49	47
小	small	16	13	10	15	11	2	101	76	38
	tiny	2	0	2	7	1	3	14	3	12
	little	39	23	29	65	14	50	75	46	30

我们一一分析各形容词的共现频率。

"大—big"共现："大—big"共现情况在《聊斋志异》的大中华译本与鲁迅小说的杨译本中较为典型，均多于其所对应的母语译者译本，其中，杨译本与蓝译本悬殊较大，多 32 次。《红楼梦》的两译本差距不大。

"大—large"共现："大—large"共现率在三对译本各不相同，《聊斋志异》的母语译者译本多，鲁迅小说的非母语译者译本多，《红楼梦》两译本相当。

"大—great"共现:"大—great"共现情况在《聊斋志异》的母语译者译本中较多,其他两对译本中相当。

"小—small"共现:《红楼梦》和鲁迅小说的译本中,非母语译者译本的"小—small"共现率均多于母语译者译本,该数据在《聊斋志异》的两译本中相当。

"小—tiny"共现:3对译本中,母语译者译本的"小—tiny"的共现频次均高于非母语译者译本,其中鲁迅小说蓝译本和杨译本差距最大。

"小—little"共现:《红楼梦》和《聊斋志异》的译本中,非母语译者译本的"小—little"共现率均高于母语译者译本,该数据在《红楼梦》两译本中相当。

总体而言,上表中的语料库共现数据表明,母语译者在表达"大"和"小"的意思时,相对非母语译者而言,更加倾向于选择 great,tiny,little 等情感色彩较为浓厚的词语,而避开 big,small 等中性词语。

四、描写性形容词

如前所述,描写性形容词(descriptive adjective),又称为非限制性形容词,作进一步描绘之用,即便省去,也不影响被修饰词的本义。带有某些形容词后缀的形容词是较为典型的描写性形容词。我们将《红楼梦》、鲁迅小说以及《聊斋志异》的3对译本中的相关形容词加以统计,具体统计对象为25类描写性形容词。

表5.9 各译本描写性形容词使用统计

序号	后缀	《红楼梦》		鲁迅小说		《聊斋志异》	
		霍译本	杨译本	蓝译本	杨译本	闵译本	大中华译本
1	-able	105	34	117	113	113	56
2	-ible	28	5	39	43	29	13
3	-al	126	89	319	299	214	172
4	-an	0	0	6	2	0	0
5	-ian	1	1	14	7	1	0
6	-ant	35	21	47	54	25	25
7	-ent	73	42	122	109	61	52
8	-ar	19	25	59	57	24	17
9	-ary	21	4	45	50	35	16
10	-ed	188	134	330	327	164	175

（续表）

序号	后缀	《红楼梦》		鲁迅小说		《聊斋志异》	
		霍译本	杨译本	蓝译本	杨译本	闵译本	大中华译本
11	-en	53	35	140	140	78	73
12	-ern	2	3	22	21	15	11
13	-ese	2	0	25	30	0	6
14	-ful	66	22	63	121	73	67
15	-ic	28	20	67	40	22	17
16	-ical	12	4	32	29	23	7
17	-ing	96	52	114	109	97	66
18	-ish	9	7	13	15	6	10
19	-ist	18	24	5	8	28	21
20	-ive	25	13	53	48	27	19
21	-less	41	40	67	71	41	16
22	-ly	71	34	121	96	68	61
23	-ous	121	75	168	130	94	78
24	-some	6	6	5	6	12	14
25	-ward	0	1	1	6	6	0
	合计	322	187	576	531	342	299

从上述数据来看，母语译者译本的该类形容词数量均超过非母语译者译本。

我们具体统计、对比数据悬殊较大《红楼梦》霍译本与杨译本中的-able形容词使用。具体如下表。

表5.10 《红楼梦》霍译本和杨译本-able形容词使用对比

霍译本			杨译本		
类符数：49			类符数：14		
形符数：105			形符数：34		
No.	Word	Freq.	No.	Word	Freq.
1	able	32	1	able	14
2	unable	14	2	unable	5
3	agreeable	5	3	capable	3
4	uncomfortable	4	4	valuable	2
5	miserable	3	5	agreeable	1
6	comfortable	2	6	amiable	1
7	considerable	2	7	charitable	1
8	valuable	2	8	considerable	1
9	adorable	1	9	deplorable	1
10	affable	1	10	favourable	1
11	amiable	1	11	honourable	1

第五章　形容词使用对比

（续表）

霍译本			杨译本		
12	available	1	12	marriageable	1
13	capable	1	13	miserable	1
14	charitable	1	14	unpredictable	1
15	considerable	1			
16	dependable	1			
17	disagreeable	1			
18	honourable	1			
19	impressionable	1			
20	incapable	1			
21	inconsiderable	1			
22	inconsolable	1			
23	indefatigable	1			
24	indescribable	1			
25	innumerable	1			
26	insufferable	1			
27	invariable	1			
28	liable	1			
29	memorable	1			
30	minable	1			
31	observable	1			
32	palpable	1			
33	pitiable	1			
34	pleasurable	1			
35	presentable	1			
36	reasonable	1			
37	recuperable	1			
38	reliable	1			
39	remarkable	1			
40	seasonable	1			
41	suitable	1			
42	traceable	1			
43	unaccountable	1			
44	unanswerable	1			
45	unapproachable	1			
46	unavoidable	1			
47	unconscionable	1			
48	uncontrollable	1			
49	unutterable	1			

从上表中可以看出，霍译本使用 49 种共 105 例带 -able 后缀的形容词，杨译本使用 14 种共 34 例该类形容词，二者种类和数量均悬殊巨大。两译本中 able 与 unable 出现频次分别为 46 和 19，去除这两词后，霍译本与杨译本该类形容词数据分别为 47 种 59 例，12 种 15 例。

五、最高级形容词

形容词分原形、比较级与最高级，最高级常用作英语的夸张修辞手法。我们比较一下 5 对译本中最高级形容词的使用情况，统计如下。

表 5.11 各译本最高级形容词使用对比

原文	《聊斋志异》		《红楼梦》		鲁迅小说		《骆驼祥子》		《浮生六记》	
译本	大中华译本	闵译本	杨译本	霍译本	杨译本	蓝译本	施译本	葛译本	林译本	拜伦译本
最高级形容词	33	60	46	80	133	140	119	147	45	54

上表显示，5 对译本中，母语译者均比非母语译者使用了更多的最高级形容词，这说明了两类译本之间有系统性差异。其中，《红楼梦》两译本差距最大，二者相差 34 个。

最高级形容词大致有三种功能：(1) 表示专有名词；(2) 如实表达修饰程度；(3) 夸张修辞。

(1) 专有名词，如"进士"。如下例。

原文：后公举<u>进士</u>，任肥丘。

大中华译本：Some time later, Yin won the title of Jinshi in <u>the highest imperial examinations</u> and was appointed magistrate of Feiqiu County.

(2) 如实表达修饰程度。原文中也使用了最高级，译文如实译出。见下例。

原文：与兄<u>最</u>善，其人可依。

大中华译本：He is my <u>best friend</u> and someone you can trust with your life.

原文中"最善"译为 best friend，算是程度对等。

原文：有女郎携婢，拈梅花一枝，容华绝代，笑容可掬。

闵译本：One young lady was out walking with her maid and had just picked a spray of plum-blossom. She had **the prettiest face** imaginable, with a great beaming smile.

原文中的"容华绝代"，因有"绝"字，译为 the prettiest face 作为对等。

（3）夸张修饰。某些译例中，原文并未使用最高程度的修饰，但译文将最高级形容词作为一种修辞，起到烘托情节，刻画人物的文体作用。如下例：

原文：华艳妆出；仲睨之良久，大喜，蹈舞若狂，曰："吾悟矣！"

…and, far from keeping away, she came in to him dressed in **her finest clothes**. Zhong stared at her a long while, and then began dancing wildly for joy. "I am enlightened!"

原文中"华艳妆出"译为 her finest clothes，采用最高级形容词，为了突出其华艳之程度，烘托故事情节。

我们将《聊斋志异》闵译本与大中华译本中的最高级形容词译例，详尽列出如下。

（一）《聊斋志异》闵译本中最高级形容词译例

原文：此真非常之奇变也。

闵译本：Truly this was a **most extraordinary phenomenon**.

原文：未顾王生九思及董曰："余阅人多矣，脉之奇无如两君者……"

闵译本：…and finally came to Dong and to another friend of his, by the name of Wang Jiusi. "I have read many pulses in my time," he pronounced. "But you two gentlemen have **the strangest and most contradictory configurations** I have ever encountered."

原文：少间笼纱一簇，导新郎入。年可十七八，丰采韶秀。

闵译本：After a little while, a bevy of servants bearing gauze lanterns ushered in the groom, a handsome young man of seventeen or eighteen, of a **most distinguished appearance** and prepossessing bearing.

原文：共思此物非寒士所有，乃信之。

闵译本：They knew how poor he was, and that he was **most unlikely to** have owned such a valuable object himself, and so were obliged to believe him.

原文：既而闭户去，嘱勿咳。夜乃复至。

闵译本：Afterwards she left him and went away, closing the door behind her and bidding him not to make **the slightest sound**. That same night she returned, and so their liaison continued for a further two days.

原文：蹑迹而窗窥之，见一狞鬼，面翠色，齿如锯。

闵译本：Creeping stealthily up to a window, he peeped through and saw the **most hideous sight**, a green-faced monster, a ghoul with great jagged teeth like a saw, leaning over a human pelt, the skin of an entire human body, spread on the bed—on his bed.

原文：生曲意承迎，笑问所来。

闵译本：…and when Shican, in his **most charming manner**, asked him where he had been…

原文：脉之，惊曰："君有鬼脉，病在少阴，不自慎者殆矣！"

闵译本：…but when the physician took his pulses he exclaimed in alarm, "Your pulse shows a spirit possession! The illness is deep in the Shao-yin Meridian. If you do not exercise **the greatest caution**, I fear for your life!"

原文：……曰："曩不实言，今魂气已游墟莽，秦缓何能为力？"

闵译本："The other day," said Dr Qi, "you were not telling me the truth, were you? Your soul is already roaming in the wilderness of death. Even **the best physician** in the world would be of no avail now!"

原文：人必力士，鸟道乃敢生开……

闵译本：Only **the mightiest warrior** can penetrate that tiny bird-track!

原文：近扶之，亦不羞缩。

闵译本：When he went to help her up, she seemed not **in the least** ashamed of her nakedness.

原文：过数日，两窗尽塞无少明，已，乃合泥涂壁孔，终日营营，不惮其劳。

闵译本：After a few days of this, both his mother's windows were completely bricked up, and not a ray of sunlight could find its way into her bedroom. Next he plastered over **the slightest chink** in the walls with mud, working at it flat out all day.

原文：少年细诘行踪，意怜之，劝设帐授徒。

闵译本：The young man, for his part, asked Kong in some detail about his own predicament and seemed **most sympathetic** to his plight. He encouraged him to set himself up as a tutor and start a little school.

原文：当晚，谈笑甚欢，即留共榻。

闵译本：The two continued to spend a **most convivial evening** together and ended up sharing the same bed that night.

原文：内一盗识兵，逡巡告曰："闻君刀最快，斩首无二割。"

闵译本：One of them recognized the soldier with the sharp sword. "Everyone says you've got **the sharpest sword**," he mumbled. "They say it can cut a head clean off in a single blow."

原文：娶三日，谓人曰："男女居室，天下之至秽，我实不为乐！"遂去妻。

闵译本：Three days after the wedding he said to one of his acquaintances, "The act of love performed by a man and a woman is surely **the vilest thing** in the world! I find no pleasure in it!" Consequently he rid himself of his wife.

原文：里党乞求不靳与……

闵译本：If a neighbour begged from him, he gave him whatever it was he wanted without **the least hesitation**.

原文：及仲蹇落，存问绝少，仲旷达不为意。

闵译本：But now that he was down and out, hardly a single one of them showed **the slightest concern** for him. Zhong adopted a philosophical view of this, and refused to take offence.

原文：计两全者，无如从君，是以不惮千里。

闵译本：After much reflection I have decided that **the best thing** is to be with you. So I have travelled all this way to join you.

原文：华艳妆出；仲睨之良久，大喜，蹈舞若狂，曰："吾悟矣！"

闵译本：…and, far from keeping away, she came in to him dressed in **her finest clothes**. Zhong stared at her a long while, and then began dancing wildly for joy. "I am enlightened!"

原文：俄，一贵官出，迎见生甚恭，既登堂，生启问曰："素既不叙，遽疏参谒。

闵译本：Presently a distinguished-looking mandarin came forward to meet them, greeting Dou very politely and escorting him up into a reception hall. "This is **most kind** of you," said Dou. "But I do not have the honour of knowing who you are, and have never called on you before, so I can not help but feel some what ill at ease."

原文：贵官曰："寡君以先生清族世德，倾风结慕，深愿思晤焉。"

闵译本："My lord and master," replied the mandarin, "has long heard of you as a man of excellent family and **the highest principles**. He is most anxious to make your acquaintance."

原文："王起曰：见君子，实惬心好，何仓卒而便言离也？卿既不住，亦无敢于强，若烦萦念，更当再邀。"

闵译本："I am **most delighted** to have met you," replied the King, rising to his feet, "and I am only sorry that you are in such a hurry to leave. But I will not detain you. If you care to remember us, I shall be very glad to invite you here again."

原文：生曰："有卿在目，真使人乐而忘死。"

闵译本："Having you by my side, **my dearest**, " he said to the Princess, 'brings me such joy that I could forget death itself.

原文：章曰："含香殿大学士臣黑翼，为非常怪异，祈早迁都，以存国脉事。"

第五章　形容词使用对比

闵译本：The document began: From the Grand Secretary of State, Black Wings, of the Hall of Contained Fragrance, to His Royal Majesty, announcing the arrival of a **most strange monster**. We advise the immediate evacuation of the Court in order to ensure the very survival of your kingdom.

原文：于惊起，视之，绿衣长裙，婉妙无比。

闵译本：He jumped up in alarm, and found himself standing before a young lady of **the most incomparable delicacy** and **the most exquisite beauty**, clad in a green tunic and a long skirt.

原文：举首细视，则一蛛大如弹，挢捉一物，哀鸣声嘶。于破网挑下，去其缚缠，则一绿蜂，奄然将毙矣。

闵译本：Looking up he saw a huge spider, like a big black bolus, holding in its clutches a little creature that was making **the most pitiful noise**: it was a green hornet, in the throes of death.

原文：又或以金，非金也，乃罗刹鬼骨，留之能截取人心肝；二者，凡以投时好耳。

闵译本：Or else I tempt him with a piece of gold, which is really not gold at all but the spirit-bone of a raksha-demon. Once he has taken the gold, I can use it to cut out his heart and liver. I use whichever method seems **most likely** to work at the time.'

原文：女迎笑曰："花城娘子，贵趾久弗涉，今日西南风紧，吹送来也！小哥子抱得未？"

闵译本："It's been such an age since you last visited, **dearest Sister Flower**!" returned Butterfly, with a teasing smile. 'What Fair Wind of Love blows you here today? And have you had your little baby boy yet?'

原文：三娘见母与巧娘苦相抵，意不自安，以一身调停两间，始各挽怒为喜。

闵译本：Tertia was **most distressed** to see the two of them at each other's throats and tried her utmost to mediate, eventually succeeding in bringing them round and restoring the peace.

原文：后里舍稍闻之，共为不平，鸣于官。官械妇，妇不肯伏，收之。

闵译本：When the neighbours came to know of this, they were **most indignant** and reported the matter to the local Magistrate, who interrogated the woman under torture, and when she still refused to confess had her thrown into the county jail.

原文：意懊丧，不欲行。群鬼乱挞之，痛极而窜于野。

闵译本：He stood there looking **most woebegone** and refusing to move, whereupon the demons came behind him and lashed him until he was in such pain that he ran away from them and out into the open country.

原文：蛇人挥曰："去之！世无百年不散之筵。从此隐身大谷，必且为神龙，笥中何可以久居也？"

闵译本：The snake-charmer pushed him away. "Off you go! Sooner or later even **the finest party** has to end. Go and find yourself a hiding place down in the valley. Maybe one day you will turn into a magic dragon. Surely you don't want to stay cooped up in this basket all your life?"

原文：客惧甚，不敢作声，阴以足踏诸客。而诸客绝无少动。

闵译本：He did not dare to make a sound, but stretched out a foot and furtively kicked his companions, not one of whom made **the slightest movement** in response.

原文：村中人无有警者。欲叩主人之门，又恐迟为所及。

闵译本：Not a single villager seemed to hear, and he did not dare to stop and rouse the landlord by knocking at the inn door, for fear that **the slightest delay** might result in his capture by the fiend.

原文：烛之死，然心下丝丝有动气。

闵译本：They shone a lamp on him, and though at first he seemed dead, when they felt his heart they detected **the faintest trace** of a pulse.

原文：……炊烟起而人声杂矣。讶之，投刺往谒。翁趋出，逆而入，笑语可亲。

第五章　形容词使用对比

闵译本：Astonished to see smoke rising from a chimney and to hear voices coming from within, he sent in his visiting card, whereupon the old man came hurrying out and welcomed him very civilly, smiling and chattering in a **most affable manner**.

原文：既归，遣人馈遗其家；翁犒赐丰隆。

闵译本：When Li returned home, he sent one of his servants with presents for the old man, who gave the servant a **most generous tip**.

原文：俄见一少女经门外过，望见王，秋波频顾，眉目含情，仪容娴婉。

闵译本：Then, the next minute, another young woman passed fleetingly by the doorway and catching sight of Wang cast him a bewitching glance, full of **the strangest tenderness and passion**.

原文：孜渐长，孔武有力，喜田猎，不务生产，乐斗好杀。

闵译本：As Little Wang grew up he showed a great liking for physical activities, especially hunting and combat of all sorts, and was not in **the least squeamish** when it came to taking life.

原文：孜承奉甚孝；然误触之，则恶声暴吼。

闵译本：Little Wang was an extremely devoted son, but subject to **the direst rages and tantrums** if crossed.

原文：女以亲迎为期。宿以为远，又请。女厌纠缠，约待病愈。

闵译本：Su protested that this was unbearably far in the future and insisted on something sooner, whereupon Rouge, finding his pestering **most disagreeable**, eventually relented and agreed to see him again once she was fully recovered.

原文：公固疑是毛，至此益信。施以毒刑，尽吐其实。

闵译本：That was how the Judge confirmed his suspicions of Big Mao, who was now subjected to **the harshest torture** and confessed to everything.

原文：若毛大者：刁猾无籍，市井凶徒。

闵译本：As for the man known as Big Mao: he is an unscrupulous rogue, the **worst**

kind of street thug.

原文：烛之则一木偶，高大如人。弓矢尚缠腰际，刻画狰狞；剑击处，皆有血出。

闵译本：Eventually he held high his lamp and beheld before him a man-sized wooden puppet, decorated in **the most terrifying fashion**, the arrows still tied at its waist. Blood was flowing from every place where his sword had struck.

原文：李惧，匿首尸下。

闵译本：In terror, Li buried his own head under **the nearest corpse**.

原文：值科试，公游扬于学使，遂领冠军。

闵译本：When it came to the time for the preliminary examination, Ding spoke highly of Ye to the Examiner, and as a result he was ranked among **the most promising candidates**.

原文：公期望綦切，闱后索文读之，击节称叹。

闵译本：After the first-degree examination proper, Magistrate Ding, who had entertained **the highest hopes** for Ye, obtained his draft essay and was ecstatic in its praise.

原文：生甚感佩。辞而归，杜门不出。无何寝疾。

闵译本：Ye was **most grateful** to him for his solicitude, but bade him farewell and returned home, where he shut himself away, refused to go out and in a short while fell seriously ill.

原文：抵里，命子师事生，夙夜与俱。

闵译本：When they reached Ding's native village, he instructed his own son to treat Ye with **the greatest respect** and to regard him as his teacher, waiting upon him and constantly keeping him company.

原文：生惨然不乐，公不忍强，嘱公子至都为之纳粟。

闵译本：Ye seemed **most unhappy** at the idea of leaving, and Ding did not insist but instead instructed his son to purchase for Ye the rank of membership in the Imperial

College once he was in the capital, since this would entitle Ye to sit directly for the second degree.

原文：有女郎携婢，拈梅花一枝，容华绝代，笑容可掬。

闵译本：One young lady was out walking with her maid and had just picked a spray of plum-blossom. She had **the prettiest face** imaginable, with a great beaming smile.

原文：食方竟，家人捉双卫来寻生。先是，母待生久不归，始疑。

闵译本：When they had eaten, a number of his servants arrived from home with two mules, having been sent in search of their young master by his mother, who had become **most anxious** when he had failed to return.

原文：趋与语，却又蕴藉可爱。

闵译本：Yin approached him and engaged him in conversation. He found him indeed to be a **most charming and cultivated person**.

原文：尹谢之。命酒款宴，言笑甚欢。向暮，有昆仑捉马挑灯，迎导以去。

闵译本：Yin apologized for his incivility and set wine and food before his guest, whereupon they dined together in a **most convivial manner** until late in the evening, when two dark-skinned servants came with horses and lanterns to fetch their young master home.

原文：滨州一秀才，读书斋中。有款门者，启视，则皤然一翁，形貌甚古。

闵译本：There was a certain gentleman of Binzhou who was reading in his study one day when he heard a knock at the door. He opened the door and beheld a white-haired old man of a **most antique** **appearance**.

原文：一日，密祈翁曰："君爱我良厚。顾我贫若此，君但一举手，金钱宜可立致。何不小周给？"

闵译本：During one of these visits, he pleaded confidentially with him. 'You and I are such good friends now. Look at the poverty that surrounds me. I know it would be **the easiest thing** in the world for you to come by some money. Won't you help me out?'

原文：既归，灰心木坐，了不勾当家务。

闵译本：On his return home, from that day onwards he sat in a bemused state, refusing to take **the slightest part** in family affairs.

原文：寇退，家人得尸，将舁瘗之，闻其气缕缕然……

闵译本：When the bandits had gone and the family came to recover the corpse for burial, they detected **the faintest trace** of breathing, and on closer examination saw that the man's windpipe was not quite severed.

（二）《聊斋志异》大中华译本中最高级形容词

原文：然而董君实甚。

大中华译本：You, Mr. Dong, your pulse is **most extraordinary**.

原文：后公举进士，任肥丘。

大中华译本：Some time later, Yin won the title of Jinshi in **the highest imperial examinations** and was appointed magistrate of Feiqiu County.

原文：九郎曰："此何子萧，昔之名士，今之太史。与兄最善，其人可依。"

大中华译本：Huang said: "This is He Zixiao who was a famous scholar in the past and now carries the academic title of hanlin. He is my **best friend** and someone you can trust with your life."

原文：九郎惊曰："两世之交，但可自效，顶踵所不敢惜。何忽作此态向人？"

大中华译本：Huang was surprised, saying: "We've been **the best of friends**. If there's anything I can do for you, just tell me. Why do you have to act like this?"

原文：过数日，两窗尽塞，无少明。已乃合泥涂壁孔，终日营营，不惮其劳。

大中华译本：This went on for a few days until the two windows were fully blocked and there was not **the least bit of light** left in the room. Then he started to mix earth with water and, using the mud, blocked the small holes in the wall. He busied himself the whole day, not minding being tired at all.

原文：母出非望，又睹美妇，方共忻慰。

大中华译本：His mother was delighted by his surprise return and found her daughter-in-law **most charming**. The three were overjoyed at their reunion.

原文：后生举进士，授延安司李……

大中华译本：Later, Xueli passed **the highest imperial examination** and became a jinshi and was put in charge of all the criminal cases in Yan'an Prefecture in Shaanxi Province.

原文：生请与吴郎俱，又虑翁媪不肯离幼子，终日议不果。

大中华译本：Xueli invited her and her husband to go with them, but Jiaona was afraid her parents-in-law would miss **their youngest son**. They discussed the matter for a whole day without finding any solution.

原文：公方悟，顿首泣曰："辱膺宠命，何敢多辞？

大中华译本：Only then did Master Song realize what was happening. He bumped his head pleadingly on the floor and sobbed: "Since you deign to grant me your **most partial appointment**, how dare I stubbornly decline?

原文：内一盗识兵，逡巡告曰："闻君刀最快，斩首无二割。

大中华译本：One of them knew that soldier. He pleaded with him pitifully, saying, "I've heard that your knife is **the sharpest**. There's never a need to strike twice when you chop off a head.

原文：抵家，自诩遇仙，坚壁所不能阻，妻不信。

大中华译本：Arriving back home, Wang boasted that he had met an immortal, and now, not even **the thickest wall** could prevent him from passing through. His wife wouldn't believe him.

原文：娶三日，谓人曰："男女居室，天下之至秽，我实不为乐！"遂去妻。

大中华译本：On the third day of his marriage, he complained: "what husbands and wives do together is **the dirtiest thing** in the world. I cannot find any happiness in it!" So he drove away his wife.

原文：王命向生展拜，曰："此即莲花小女也。"

大中华译本：The king told the princess to bow to Mr. Dou and then said to Dou: "This is my youngest daughter, Lotus Flower."

原文：生曰："有卿在目，真使人乐而忘死。

大中华译本：Dou said: "With you, I am **the happiest man** in the world."

原文：真千古未见之凶，万代不遭之祸！社稷宗庙，危在旦夕！乞皇上早率宫眷，速迁乐土，云云。

大中华译本：It is the **most ferocious** monster ever seen in history. The fate of the county is in danger. We appeal to the king to take family members and palace subordinates to move to a peaceful place.

原文：公主曰："此大安宅，胜故国多矣。"

大中华译本：The princess said: "This is **the most secure place**, much better than the palace."

原文：士人曰："此间无房主，仆亦侨居。能甘荒落，旦晚惠教，幸甚。"

大中华译本：The scholar said, "There's no caretaker here. I'm a temporary tenant, too. Since you don't mind the wilderness and solitude, I would be **most fortunate** to have you teach me in the morning and evening."

原文：后数年，宁果登进士。女举一男。

大中华译本：A few years later, Ning Caichen passed the imperial examination at **the highest level** and became jinshi while Xiaoqian gave birth to a baby boy.

原文：心惊喜，如乍膺九锡。

大中华译本：He was so astonished and elated that it was like being bestowed **the highest awards** or having a title of high official conferred on him by the emperor himself.

原文：三娘见母与巧娘苦相抵，意不自安，以一身调停两间，始各挠怒为喜。

大中华译本：The exchange of unfriendly remarks between the two made Sanniang very uneasy. She tried **her best** to mediate between them, making everyone happy in the end.

原文：华姑排止之，便曳生出。

大中华译本：Huagu tried **her best** to stop their tears and dragged Lian outside.

原文：其人应命方兴，问："作何剧？"堂上相顾数语，吏下宣问所长。

大中华译本：As the man got ready to play, he asked, "What act shall I perform?" The officials spoke a few sentences among themselves. A clerk came down and proclaimed their wish to know his **best trick**.

原文：东昌卞氏，业牛医者，有女小字胭脂，才姿惠丽。

大中华译本：Yanzhi was **the youngest daughter** of Mr, Bian, a veterinarian from Dongchang, Shandong, and was known for her talents and beauty.

原文：妾向与同里，故识之，世间男子无其温婉。

大中华译本：I used to be his neighbor and that's how I got to know him. He is **the most understanding man** in the world.

原文：崇祯间，殿试在都，仆疫不起，患之。

大中华译本：During the reign of Chongzhen, towards the end of the Ming Dynasty, he went to the capital city to take part in **the highest imperial examination**. While he was there, his servant caught an illness and took to his bed. Yu became very worried.

原文：文章词赋，冠绝当时，而所遇不偶，困于名场。

大中华译本：Although he was **the most outstanding literary talent** in the county, his luck always proved fickle and he failed the imperial civil service examination repeatedly.

原文：公遗问不绝，而服药百裹，殊罔所效。

大中华译本：Ding sent his envoy to visit him and brought him medicine, money and other goods. But after a hundred doses of the medicine, Ye's health had **not** turned **in the least** for the better.

原文：生曰："以犬马病，劳夫子久待，万虑不宁。今幸可从杖履。"

大中华译本：To his inquiry about his health, Ye said, "It has made me feel **most uneasy** that you should have waited so long on account of my illness. Fortunately, I am now able to accompany you on the journey."

原文：公子又捷南宫，授部中主政，携生赴监，与共晨夕。

大中华译本：Shortly afterwards, the son passed **the highest imperial examination** and was given a post on the Board of Rites. He took Ye Sheng along to his official residence where they stayed together.

原文：欲呼姨氏，顾从无还往，惧有讹误。

大中华译本：He could say he wanted to call on his aunt, but they had never had any contact before. What if he was mistaken? It would be **most embarrassing**.

原文：母促令出，始极力忍笑，又面壁移时，方出。

大中华译本：When Wang's mother urged her to go out and greet the guest, she tried **her best** to keep from laughing, standing with her face to the wall for quite a while before coming out.

原文：众莫之测。母令与少女同寝止，昧爽即来省问，操女红精巧绝伦。

大中华译本：No one could figure out what was behind all this. Wang's mother arranged for Yingning to sleep with **her youngest daughter**. At daybreak, Yingning would get up and pay her respects to Wang's mother. Her needlework was exquisite.

原文：甚而父子兄弟，较尽锱铢。

大中华译本：In **the worst cases** fathers, sons, and brothers count every last dram and grain against each other.

本章小结

本章对母语译者与非母语译者的形容词使用做了对比。

（1）总体对比。整体来看，母语译者所使用形容词的绝对数量比非母语译者少，但母语译者形容词使用类别更加丰富。值得注意的是，《浮生六记》的林译本所使用的形容词在数量和类别上均多于母语译者译本。

（2）强调形容词。我们通过对比五种强调性形容词在两类译本中的使用后发现，母语译者中该类形容词的使用均高于非母语译者，表明母语译者更倾向于使用强调形容词。我们通过进一步对比鲁迅小说的蓝译本与杨译本中 own 的使用后发现，从数量与翻译方法上来看，蓝译本更倾向于使用 own 来强调，翻译策略也更加灵活。

（3）形容词情感色彩对比。我们统计了两类译本中表示大、小的形容词的使用后发现，总体而言，母语译者译本比非母语译者译本更多使用情感色彩更加浓厚的形容词。

（4）描写性形容词。数据统计对比发现，母语译者译本更倾向于使用该类形容词。

（5）最高级形容词。经数据对比发现，母语译者较之非母语译者更倾向于使用最高级形容词。

第六章　副词使用对比

　　副词指用以修饰动词、形容词、其他副词以及全句的词，可表时间、地点、程度、方式等概念（薄冰，2000）。副词的分类在各类语法书中标准不一，名称也不同。薄冰（2000）按照意义将副词分为方式副词、地点副词、方向副词、时间副词和强调副词，又按照功能将其分为句子副词、连接副词、解释性副词、关系副词、缩合连接副词、疑问副词和感叹副词。张道真（2002）将副词分为时间副词、地点副词、方式副词、程度副词、强调副词、疑问副词、连接副词、关系副词和句子副词。Alexander（1988）将副词分为方式副词（adverb of manner）、地点副词（adverb of place）、时间副词（adverb of time）、频度副词（adverb of frequency）、程度副词（adverb of degree）、强化副词（intensifier）、焦点副词（adverb of focus）、观点副词（viewpoint adverb）和连接词（connectives）。还有一些词典书（如剑桥在线词典）提出类似观点副词和句子副词的一类副词，即评价副词（evaluative adverb）。

　　和前面章节所讨论的名词、动词、形容词一样，作为主要词性之一的副词也有其独特的文体内涵，值得挖掘。在本章中，我们将统计、分析5对译本的总体副词特征，并聚焦3类副词：程度副词、方式副词、否定副词。

一、副词整体特征

　　5对译本副词统计如下：

第六章 副词使用对比

表 6.1 各译本副词使用统计对比

原著	译本	副词	
		数量	种类
鲁迅小说	杨译本	6614	536
	蓝译本	8148	640
《聊斋志异》	大中华译本	3974	357
	闵译本	4096	458
《红楼梦》	杨译本	3468	348
	霍译本	4598	523
《骆驼祥子》	施译本	6802	498
	葛译本	5891	454
《浮生六记》	林译本	2536	312
	拜伦译本	2771	301

根据上述数据，在鲁迅小说、《聊斋志异》以及《红楼梦》3 部著作的译本中，母语译者使用的副词数量与种类均高于非母语译者，其中，鲁迅小说的蓝译本比杨译本多使用 103 种副词，悬殊最大，闵译本较大中华译本多使用 101 种副词，霍译本较杨译本多出 75 种副词。《骆驼祥子》和《浮生六记》的译本有所不同，非母语译者使用的副词数量与种类较多，但两者差距较其他 3 对译本小。施译本和林译本分别比母语译者译本多使用 44 种和 11 种副词。平均而言，母语译者译本较非母语译者译本使用的副词种类更为丰富。

二、程度副词

英语中的程度副词用于修饰形容词或副词，是对一系列语义上可以表示程度高低的副词的总称。母语译者与非母语译者在程度副词的使用上是否会有不同，我们对相关数据进行了统计。

根据 BNC 语料库数据统计，英语中最常见的程度副词为 very 和 so。我们统计 5 对译本中这 2 个程度副词的使用分布，数据如下。

表 6.2 各译本程度副词使用统计对比

原文	鲁迅小说		《红楼梦》		《聊斋志异》		《骆驼祥子》		《浮生六记》	
程度副词	蓝译本	杨译本	霍译本	杨译本	闵译本	大中华译本	葛译本	施译本	拜伦译本	林译本
very	30	174	94	17	58	120	16	107	61	116
so	161	333	220	180	147	228	281	341	187	97

从上表统计看，5 对译本中，除了红楼梦译本，其他 4 对中的非母语译者均比母语译者使用更多 very，其中鲁迅小说两译本差距最大，杨译本较蓝译本多出 144 个。so 的使用分布与 very 大致相当，不过拜伦译本与霍译本一样，比非母语译者使用频率更高。平均看来，非母语译者更偏爱使用这两个高频程度副词。这一数据对比可能意味着，在翻译原文的程度副词时，非母语译者的处理手段可能相对单一。

我们以鲁迅小说蓝译本和杨译本为对象，检索原文中频率最高的程度副词"非常"和"极"的英译方法。原文程度副词共有 82 处，其英译有以下 3 种方法：对等、变换和省略。对等即同样使用程度副词如 very，so，most，extremely 等做对等的处理，例如：

原文：他极小心的，幽静的，一锄一锄往下掘……

译文：**Very** carefully and quietly he dug down, stroke by stroke….

变换即将原文中的程度副词翻译成其他语法形式，如程度形容词或双重否定等，例如：

原文：这王胡，又癞又胡，别人都叫他王癞胡，阿 Q 却删去了一个癞字，然而非常渺视他。

译文：Now although – for his own delicate reasons – Ah-Q preferred not to bring up the subject of ringworm, this Wang still enjoyed his **utter** contempt.

省略即在译文中对原文中的程度副词做了省略处理。我们分别统计各译本两种策略的使用情况。

（一）蓝译本英译策略

1. 蓝译本对等策略译例

蓝译本程度副词采取对等翻译策略的译例有 18 例，共使用 13 种表达

第六章　副词使用对比

程度的副词或副词词组：a great，all too，deeply，enough，indeed，most，much，obviously，particularly，perfectly，quite，unusually，utterly，very。译例如下：

（1）a great （1例）

原文：他议论非常多，而且往往颇奇警。

蓝译本：He had **a great** many views on all kinds of subjects – many of them startlingly acute.

（2）all too （1例）

原文：……它的食量，在我们其实早是一个极易觉得的很重的负担。

蓝译本：…his appetite became a heavy daily burden of which we were **all too** conscious.

（3）deeply （1例）

原文：她当时并不回答什么话，但大约非常苦闷了……

蓝译本：Though she said nothing, Xianglin's wife was left **deeply** troubled by Mrs Liu's advice.

（4）enough （1例）

原文：我去卖棺材虽然有些离奇，但只要价钱极便宜，原铺子就许要，至少总可以捞回几文酒钱来。

蓝译本：Though it was bound to look odd, the store I'd originally bought it off would probably take it back, as long as I kept my price low **enough**. I'd get back a few coppers to go drinking with, at least.

（5）indeed （2例）

原文：孔子曰，"名不正则言不顺"。这原是应该极注意的。

蓝译本：As Confucius says: "If a name is not right, the words will not ring true." Wise words **indeed**.

原文：……但觉得有学问的七爷这么说，事情自然非常重大，无可挽回……

蓝译本：But they could see that if a man of Mr Zhao's wisdom was talking like this, then the situation was serious **indeed**; beyond salvation, in fact.

（6）most（2例）

原文：（海乙那）时常吃死肉，连极大的骨头，都细细嚼烂，咽下肚子去，想起来也教人害怕。

蓝译本：…with terrifying eyes and a fondness for dead meat, capable of chewing the **most** enormous bones down to a pulp. I shiver just to think of it.

原文：我们总算度过了极难忍受的冬天，这北京的冬天……

蓝译本：This **most** insufferable of Beijing winters — we had survived it.

（7）much（1例）

原文：过了十多日，七斤从城内回家，看见他的女人非常高兴。

蓝译本：One evening, however, some ten days later, Seven-Pounds returned home to find his wife in **much**-improved.

（8）obviously（1例）

原文：我生平没有吃过荞麦粉，这回一尝，实在不可口，却是非常甜。

蓝译本：It was the first time I'd had buckwheat, and I didn't like the taste much, even though there was **obviously** a lot of sugar in it.

（9）particularly（2例）

原文：我给那些因为在近旁而极响的爆竹声惊醒。

蓝译本：I woke with a start to a **particularly** raucous blaze of firecrackers near by.

原文：子君有怨色，在早晨，极冷的早晨，这是从未见过的，但也许是从我看来的怨色。

蓝译本：One morning – one **particularly** cold morning – Zijun woke up with a look of sour grievance I had never seen before; or perhaps I only imagined it.

（10）perfectly（1例）

原文：他们订有四十多条条约，非常详细，所以非常平等，十分自由。

蓝译本：Forty clauses in their prenuptial agreement, to make sure everything's good and clear, and **perfectly** free and equal.

（11）quite（1例）

原文：——好<u>极</u>好极。

蓝译本：First class, **quite** first class.

（12）unusually（1例）

原文：我辞别连殳出门的时候，圆月已经升在中天了，是<u>极</u>静的夜。

蓝译本：I said goodnight to Lianshu at the door and emerged into an **unusually** still night, a full moon shining directly overhead.

（13）utterly（1例）

原文：大王是向来善于猜疑，又<u>极</u>残忍的。

蓝译本：Our king is by nature suspicious – and **utterly** ruthless.

（14）very（2例）

原文：我看她时，她的眼睛也注视我，而且口角上渐渐增多了笑影：我知道她一定也是<u>极其</u>爱我的。

蓝译本：When I looked at her, she seemed to gaze back at me, her lips curling into a smile; I knew that she loved me **very** much.

原文：然而这一回，她的境遇却改变得<u>非常</u>大。

蓝译本：And yet she seemed **very** different.

2. 蓝译本变换策略译例

蓝译本程度副词采取的变换翻译策略可细分为两种情况：一是处理为表示程度的形容词或类似结构；二是词汇语义具体化，即使用语义更加具体的词汇或语法结构，以将原文副词所表示的程度内涵包括在内。

（1）表示程度的形容词（6例）

蓝译本共有6个使用形容词对应原文程度副词的译例，涉及8个形容词或类似结构：absolute, extra, perfect, unimpugnable, unusual, utter, such a, what a。译例如下：

原文：下了一天雪，到夜还没有止，屋外一切静<u>极</u>，静到要听出静的声音来。

蓝译本：Snow had fallen all day and deep into the night. Outside, the quiet was so **absolute** you could almost hear it.

原文：我只好极小心，照例连吸烟卷的烟也谨防飞散。

蓝译本：Now, **extra** precautions in my daily life became necessary – permitting my cigarette smoke to escape through the window once more became unacceptably risky.

原文：从这荷池里，虽然从来没有见过养出半朵荷花来，然而养虾蟆却实在是一个极合式的处所。

蓝译本：Although the lotus had never taken, the pond looked a **perfect** home for the tadpoles.

原文：我所聊以自慰的，是还有一个"阿"字非常正确，绝无附会假借的缺点，颇可以就正于通人。

蓝译本：My only consolation in this whole sorry business is that one syllable of his name at least – "Ah" – can boast of an **unimpugnable** correctness.

原文：独有眼睛非常大，睫毛也很长……

蓝译本：It was just her eyes that were **unusual**: enormous, with very long lashes…

原文：阿Q却删去了一个癞字，然而非常渺视他。

蓝译本：Now although – for his own delicate reasons – Ah-Q preferred not to bring up the subject of ringworm, this Wang still enjoyed his **utter** contempt.

原文："说不清"是一句极有用的话。

蓝译本："I don't really know" – **what a** useful little phrase it is.

原文：那时人说：因为伊，这豆腐店的买卖非常好。

蓝译本：Everyone used to say back then that it was thanks to her the bean-curd shop turned over **such a** tidy profit.

（2）语义具体化（11例）

如前所述，语义具体化即使用语义更加具体的词语或表达，将原文的程度内涵涵盖进去。蓝译本共有12处采取语义具体化策略。译例如下：

原文：他又觉得很可怜，仿佛自己作了大恶似的，<u>非常</u>难受。

蓝译本：Again, he was paralysed by pity, **agonized** by the enormity of his act.

Agonize 本身即有"十分痛苦"之意。

原文："四翁！"外面的暗中忽然起了<u>极响</u>的叫喊。

蓝译本："Siming, old chap!" a voice **boomed** out of the darkness.

上例中，boom 一词本身便暗含了响声的程度，无需再加程度副词。

原文：他心里但觉得事情似乎十分危急，也想想些方法，想些计划，但总是<u>非常模糊</u>，贯穿不得："辫子呢辫子？丈八蛇矛。"

蓝译本：Though he could sense the situation was critical, every attempt to find a solution **fizzled out**: "Where's your queue?"

Fizzle out 指"消失"，可指模糊程度之高。

原文：他兴高采烈得<u>非常</u>："天门两块！"

蓝译本：He was **dizzy with** euphoria. "Two dollar on Heaven's Gate!"

上例中，euphoria 即表示高兴程度之甚，涵盖了非常之义。

原文：他这一夜睡得<u>非常</u>晚。

蓝译本：Sleep eluded him until **far into** the night.

Far into 这个形容词+介词结构可对应原文时间。

原文：四铭接来看时，知道是字典，但文字<u>非常</u>小，又是横行的。

蓝译本：When he'd taken the book from his son, Siming realized it was a dictionary with **tiny**, horizontal print.

原文：人们真是可笑的动物，一点<u>极</u>微末的小事情，便会受着很深的影响。

蓝译本：What foolish creatures we humans are, allowing such **tiny** things to worry us.

以上两例中，tiny 含有"非常、极"之意。

原文：伊便知道这一定是皇帝坐了龙庭，而且一定须有辫子，而且七斤一定是<u>非常</u>危险。

蓝译本：She now knew for sure that the emperor was back on the throne, that queues were an essential requirement once more, and that Seven-Pounds was in **mortal** danger.

上例中，mortal 意为"致命的"，对应原文语境中的"非常"。

原文：因为雌的一匹的奶非常多，却并不见有进去哺养孩子的形迹。

蓝译本：…though the female was **swollen with** milk, she never seemed to go down into the burrow to feed her children.

上例中，swollen with milk 意指奶水多到身体发胀，即奶水非常多。

原文：这一回她的变化非常大。

蓝译本：This – this **transformed** her.

Transform 即指非常巨大的变化。

原文：他极小心的，幽静的，一锄一锄往下掘，然而深夜究竟太寂静了，尖铁触土的声音，总是钝重的不肯瞒人的发响。

蓝译本：He dug **as** carefully and quietly **as he could**, but the regular thump of iron blade on earth reverberated through the still night.

As...as...could 短语即指程度之甚，对应原文的程度副词。

（二）杨译本英译策略

1. 杨译本对等策略译例

杨译本程度副词采取对等翻译策略的案例有41例，共使用14种表达程度的副词或副词词组：absolutely, all too, bitterly, enough, extremely, greatly, highly, most, much, really, so, thoroughly, unusually, very。译例如下：

（1）absolutely（1例）

原文：我所聊以自慰的，是还有一个"阿"字非常正确……

杨译本：The only thing that consoles me is the fact that the character "Ah" is **absolutely** correct.

（2）all too（1例）

原文：它的食量，在我们其实早是一个极易觉得的很重的负担。

杨译本：His appetite had long been a heavy liability, of which we were **all too** conscious.

（3）bitterly（2例）

原文：在早晨，<u>极</u>冷的早晨，这是从未见过的，但也许是从我看来的怨色。

杨译本：This happened for the first time one morning, one **bitterly** cold morning, or so I imagined.

原文：她<u>非常</u>后悔，不由的自己说……

杨译本：She repented **bitterly**, and found herself saying: …

（4）enough（1例）

原文：但只要价钱<u>极</u>便宜，原铺子就许要，至少总可以捞回几文酒钱来。

杨译本：…still, if the price were low **enough** the shop from which I bought it would have taken it, and at least I could have saved a little money for wine.

（5）extremely（1例）

原文：……但觉得有学问的七爷这么说，事情自然<u>非常</u>重大，无可挽回……

杨译本：…but they supposed that since the learned Mr. Chao said this, the situation must be **extremely** serious, irrevocable in fact.

（6）greatly（1例）

原文：不料六一公公竟<u>非常</u>感激起来，将大拇指一翘，得意的说道……

杨译本：To my surprise, the old man was **greatly** pleased. He stuck up a thumb, and declared with satisfaction…

（7）highly（1例）

原文：听说他还对母亲<u>极</u>口夸奖我，说："小小年纪便有见识，将来一定要中状元。"

杨译本：I heard he had praised me **highly** to mother, saying, "He's so young, yet he knows what's what. He's sure to pass all the official examinations in future."

（8）most（6例）

原文：孔子曰，"名不正则言不顺"。这原是应该<u>极</u>注意的。

杨译本：Confucius said, "If the name is not correct, the words will not ring true"; and this axiom should be **most** scrupulously observed.

原文：但他对于"男女之大防"却历来非常严……

杨译本：…he had always shown himself **most** scrupulous in observing "strict segregation of the sexes"…

原文：他先恭维我不去索薪，不肯亲领，非常之清高，一个人正应该这样做……

杨译本：First he praised me for not going to demand payment and refusing to fetch my pay, calling me **most** high-minded, a fine example to others.

原文：见我毫不热心，便又叹一口气，显出极惋惜的样子。

杨译本：…but when he saw how indifferent I was, he sighed and looked **most** disappointed.

原文：虽然从来没有见过养出半朵荷花来，然而养虾蟆却实在是一个极合式的处所。

杨译本：Although no one had ever seen even half a lotus growing there, it was a **most** appropriate place to raise frogs.

原文："说不清"是一句极有用的话。

杨译本："I am not sure" is a **most** useful phrase.

（9）much （1例）

原文：秀才听了这"庭训"，非常之以为然，便即刻撤消了驱逐阿Q的提议……

杨译本：The successful candidate, **much** impressed by this parental instruction, immediately withdrew his proposal for driving Ah Q away…

（10）really （2例）

原文：我在苦恼中常常想，说真实自然须有极大的勇气的……

杨译本：I often felt, in my depression, that **really** great courage was needed to tell the truth…

第六章　副词使用对比

原文：我生平没有吃过荞麦粉，这回一尝，实在不可口，却是<u>非常</u>甜。

杨译本：In all my life I had never eaten this buckwheat gruel, and now that I tasted it, it was **really** unpalatable, though extremely sweet.

（11）so（2例）

原文：但<u>非常</u>忧愁，忘却了吸烟……

杨译本：…sat on the doorsill smoking; but he was still **so** worried he forgot to pull on the pipe…

原文：下了一天雪，到夜还没有止，屋外一切静<u>极</u>，静到要听出静的声音来。

杨译本：It had been snowing all day, and the snow had not stopped by evening. Outside was **so** still, you could almost hear the sound of stillness.

（12）thoroughly（1例）

原文：我只觉得我四面有看不见的高墙，将我隔成孤身，使我<u>非常</u>气闷……

杨译本：I only felt that all round me was an invisible high wall, cutting me off from my fellows, and this depressed me **thoroughly**.

（13）unusually（1例）

原文：后来她也长得并不好看，不过是平常的瘦瘦的瓜子脸，黄脸皮；独有眼睛<u>非常</u>大……

杨译本：Nor did she grow up to be pretty, having just an ordinary thin oval face and pale skin. Only her eyes were **unusually** large…

（14）very（20例）

原文：他<u>极</u>小心的，幽静的，一锄一锄往下掘。

杨译本：**Very** carefully and quietly he dug down, stroke by stroke.

原文：他对着浮游在碧海里似的月亮，觉得自己的身子<u>非常</u>沉重。

杨译本：As he watched the moon floating in a sapphire sea, his own limbs seemed **very** heavy.

原文：知道是字典，但文字<u>非常</u>小，又是横行的。

杨译本：He knew it was a dictionary, but the characters were **very** small and horizontally printed too.

原文：好极好极。

杨译本：**Very** good. **Very** good.

原文：他这一夜睡得非常晚。

杨译本：That night he did not sleep till **very** late.

原文：我只好极小心，照例连吸烟卷的烟也谨防飞散。

杨译本：I had to be **very** careful then. I had to take care that my cigarette smoke did not get in other people's way.

原文：那时人说：因为伊，这豆腐店的买卖非常好。

杨译本：In those days people said that, thanks to her, that beancurd shop did **very** good business.

原文：他头上是一顶破毡帽，身上只一件极薄的棉衣，浑身瑟索着……

杨译本：He wore a shabby felt cap and just one **very** thin padded jacket, with the result that he was shivering from head to foot…

原文：我问问他的景况。他只是摇头。"非常难。"

杨译本：When I asked him how things were with him, he just shook his head."In a **very** bad way."

原文：只见几件破旧而黯淡的家具，都显得极其清疏……

杨译本：…but all I could see was the old, discoloured furniture which appeared **very** scattered…

原文：那地方叫平桥村，是一个离海边不远，极偏僻的，临河的小村庄。

杨译本：It was in a place called Pingchao Village, not far from the sea, a **very** out-of-the-way little village on a river.

原文：忽然间听得一个声音，"温一碗酒。"这声音虽然极低，却很耳熟。

杨译本：…when I heard a voice: "Warm a bowl of wine." The voice was **very** low, yet familiar.

原文：只要孩子不啼哭，是极其安闲幽静的。

杨译本：As long as the child didn't cry, it would be **very** quiet.

原文：N 显出非常得意模样，忽而又沉下脸来。

杨译本：N had been looking **very** smug. Now suddenly his face fell.

原文：房里也映得较光明，极分明的显出壁上挂着的朱拓的大"寿"字。

杨译本：The room also appeared brighter, the great red rubbing hanging on the wall showing up **very** clearly the character for Longevity.

原文："就是——"她走近两步，放低了声音，极秘密似的切切的说，"一个人死了之后，究竟有没有魂灵的？"

杨译本："It is this." She drew two paces nearer, and whispered **very** confidentially: "After a person dies, does he turn into a ghost or not?"

原文：但因为他没有家小，家中究竟非常寂寞，这大概也就是大家所谓异样之一端罢。

杨译本：Since he had neither wife nor children, however, his family was **very** quiet, and this presumably was one of the things about him considered freakish.

原文：我知道她一定也是极其爱我的。

杨译本：I knew she was **very** fond of me too.

原文：我辞别连殳出门的时候，圆月已经升在中天了，是极静的夜。

杨译本：When I left him, the full moon was high in the sky and the night was **very** still.

原文：这一回她的变化非常大。

杨译本：This time the change in her was **very** great…

2. 杨译本变换策略译例

针对原文中的部分程度副词，杨译本也采取了变换策略。与蓝译本一样，杨译本的变换策略也有两种：一为表示程度的形容词；二为其他语义具体化。

（1）表示程度的形容词（11例）

杨译本共有 11 个使用形容词对应原文程度副词的译例，涉及 11 个形容词或类似结构：a great, copious, deepest, good, great, extraordinary, largest, rare, thundering, top, what a。译例如下：

原文：然而这一回，她的境遇却改变得<u>非常</u>大。

杨译本：However, she had changed **a great** deal.

原文：因为雌的一匹的奶<u>非常</u>多，却并不见有进去哺养孩子的形迹。

杨译本：Most likely all their baby rabbits had died, because the doe had **copious** milk but showed no sign of going in to suckle her children.

原文：自己想吃人，又怕被别人吃了，都用着疑心<u>极</u>深的眼光，面面相觑。

杨译本：Wanting to eat men, at the same time afraid of being eaten themselves, they all look at each other with the **deepest** suspicion.

原文：他议论<u>非常</u>多，而且往往颇奇警。

杨译本：Once you knew him well, he was a **good** talker.

原文：伊便知道这一定是皇帝坐了龙庭，而且一定须有辫子，而且七斤一定是<u>非常</u>危险。

杨译本：She knew that an emperor must have ascended the throne, that queues must be essential again, and that Sevenpounder must be in **great** danger too.

原文：他们订有四十多条条约，<u>非常</u>详细，所以<u>非常</u>平等，十分自由。

杨译本：Their marriage contract contains over forty terms going into **great** detail, so that they have **extraordinary** equality and absolute freedom.

原文：连<u>极</u>大的骨头，都细细嚼烂，咽下肚子去，想起来也教人害怕。

杨译本：Even the **largest** bones it grinds into fragments and swallows: the mere thought of this is enough to terrify one.

原文：过了十多日，七斤从城内回家，看见他的女人<u>非常</u>高兴。

杨译本：About a fortnight later, when Sevenpounder came back from town, he found his wife in a **rare** good humour.

第六章 副词使用对比

原文:"四翁!"外面的暗中忽然起了**极**响的叫喊。

杨译本:"Ssu-min!" A **thundering** voice was heard from the darkness outside.

原文:这样的几个月之后,他们忽而自己掘土了,掘得**非常**快。

杨译本:After several months like this, they suddenly started burrowing, burrowing at **top** speed.

原文:快活**极**了,舒服极了。

杨译本:**What a** joy! Wonderful!

(2)语义具体化(1例)

如前所述,语义具体化即使用语义更加具体的词语或表达,将原文的程度内涵涵盖进去。杨译本共有1处采取语义具体化策略。译例如下:

原文:他心里但觉得事情似乎十分危急,也想想些方法,想些计画,但总是**非常**模糊,贯穿不得。

杨译本:Matters seemed to have reached a very dangerous state, and he tried to think of a way out or some plan of action. But his thoughts were **in a whirl**, and he could not straighten them out.

此例中,in a whirl 比较形象地表达了模糊程度之甚。

综上所述,鲁迅小说的蓝译本与杨译本,具体策略数据如下表所示:

表6.3 鲁迅小说蓝译本与杨译本程度副词英译策略统计

	对等	变换		省略	合计
		形容词	语义具体化		
蓝译本	19(13)	6	11	46	82
%	23.2%	20.7%		56.1%	100%
杨译本	41(14)	11	1	29	82
%	50%	14.6%		35.4%	100%

从以上案例及数据可以得出以下结论:

① 非母语译者更偏好使用对等策略,即将原文中的程度副词同样译为程度副词。这一策略在杨译本中占比50%,是蓝译本该项数据的2倍以上。

② 在使用对等翻译策略中，蓝译本共 19 例，使用了 13 个程度副词，杨译本 41 例使用了 14 种程度副词，其中 very 一词频率高达 20 次。这说明非母语译者使用的程度副词种类相对更加集中。

③ 在变化翻译策略的使用中，蓝译本共有 16 例，其中 6 项为形容词，11 项为语义具体化，而杨译本共 12 例，但语义具体化仅有 1 例。这说明蓝译本的翻译手段相对更加丰富。

三、方式副词

方式副词表示动词的行为方式，方式副词通常由形容词后加 -ly 后缀构成，如 carefully，happily，quietly，heavily 等。方式副词可修饰动词、形容词，也可以修饰副词，相比较其他类型的副词而言，所含信息量较大，修辞潜力更强。

我们统计了 5 对译本中的方式副词，统计数据如下表：

表 6.4 各译本方式副词使用统计

译本		-ly 形副词		
原著	译者	数量	种类	独特种类
鲁迅小说	杨译本	1733	341	136
	蓝译本	1483	440	235
《聊斋志异》	大中华译本	664	182	66
	闵译本	969	279	163
《红楼梦》	杨译本	467	188	66
	霍译本	930	324	202
《骆驼祥子》	施译本	1301	309	135
	葛译本	1031	269	97
《浮生六记》	林译本	494	155	80
	拜伦译本	541	150	75

从上表数据可以看出，5 对译本的方式副词分布与总体副词分布呈正相关。在鲁迅小说、《聊斋志异》以及《红楼梦》3 对译本中，母语译者使用的方式副词种类均高于非母语译者，其中，鲁迅小说的蓝译本比杨译本多使用 99 种方式副词，

闵译本较大中华译本多使用 97 种方式副词，霍译本较杨译本多出 136 种方式副词，悬殊最大。《骆驼祥子》和《浮生六记》的译本依旧与其他 3 对译本相反，非母语译者使用的方式副词种类较多，并且差距较其他 3 对译本小。施译本和林译本分别比母语译者译本多使用 38 种和 5 种方式副词。各对译本的独特方式副词也呈现同样的分布特征。平均而言，母语译者译本较非母语译者译本使用的方式副词种类更为丰富。

我们对《聊斋志异》两译本的副词所做的关键词统计，也支撑上述结论。大中华译本前 20 个相对关键词中，有 5 个是 -ly 副词，而闵译本的前 20 个相对关键词中，则有 11 个。

表 6.5 《聊斋志异》闵译本与大中华译本关键副词统计对比

No.	大中华译本			闵福德译本		
	词语	频率	关键值	词语	频率	关键值
1	n't	31	43.92	once	98	26.773
2	so	269	32.643	greatly	31	20.117
3	very	123	25.879	presently	23	20.09
4	then	245	21.653	utterly	12	16.275
5	quickly	21	15.736	eventually	22	15.742
6	just	100	13.946	but	18	14.243
7	along	8	11.334	somehow	10	13.563
8	besides	8	11.334	absolutely	9	12.207
9	only	99	10.297	newly	9	12.207
10	about	46	8.527	sooner	9	12.207
11	right	18	8.198	promptly	8	10.85
12	however	28	7.076	altogether	7	9.494
13	long	43	6.053	exactly	10	8.278
14	suddenly	57	5.998	nonetheless	10	8.278
15	cheerfully	4	5.667	most	30	7.435
16	behind	7	5.245	angrily	14	7.394
17	totally	11	5.105	ever	43	7.068

（续表）

	大中华译本			闵福德译本		
18	back	101	5.039	apart	5	6.781
19	stealthily	9	5.032	directly	5	6.781
20	as	100	4.726	duly	5	6.781

四、否定副词

否定副词，指表示否定意义的副词，英语中最常见的该类副词为 not(n't)，汉语中常见的否定副词有"不""非""未"等。否定副词是表达否定意义的一种形式。相比之下，表达否定意义时，汉语一般使用否定表达，但英语则有更多选择。李震红（2008）认为，原因之一是英语可以表示否定意义的非否定词汇较多。

我们统计、对比 5 对译本中 not 和 n't 的使用差异，并细致调查背后成因。

表 6.6　5 对译本否定副词 not 与 n't 数据对比

译本	《红楼梦》		《骆驼祥子》		鲁迅小说		《聊斋志异》		《浮生六记》	
否定副词	霍译本	杨译本	葛译本	施译本	蓝译本	杨译本	闵译本	大中华译本	拜伦译本	林译本
not	251	203	655	514	235	583	235	266	277	218
n't	0	329	0	120	34	418	0	31	6	52
合计	251	532	655	634	269	1001	235	297	283	270

从上表数据可以得出两个结论。（1）非母语译者更倾向于使用 n't。与 not 相比，其省略形式在语体上不够正式，这一观察符合两类译本的整体词汇特征；（2）总体而言，非母语译者使用该两项否定副词频率更高。这说明，母语译者使用了更多不含否定副词的否定意义表达。为了验证这一假设，我们对数据悬殊最大的鲁迅小说蓝译本与杨译本中的中文否定副词英译情况进行检索对比。我们选取原文中的"不"这一高频否定副词，检索其与 not 与 n't 的共现情况。

表 6.7　鲁迅小说否定副词"不"同蓝译本与杨译本中否定副词 not/n't 对比统计

否定副词	原文	蓝译本	杨译本
不	1226	/	/
not / n't	/	579	835

上表数据显示,原文中共有1226例否定副词"不"与译文中not与n't共现,蓝译本有579次,杨译本835次,后者显著高于前者。这进一步证明了母语译者使用了更多变的方式来表达原文否定意义。我们将蓝译本中相关表达总结如下:

(1)其他否定副词

原文:但是世事升沉无定,失意人也不会我一投名片,他便接见了。

蓝译本:But the way of the world is fickle; people down on their luck don't stay like that for ever; and so his friendships **seldom** lasted.

杨译本:However, fortune being fickle, lame dogs do **not** remain lame for ever, hence he had few steady friends.

(2)表否定意义的动词

原文:这近于盲从《新青年》,自己也很抱歉,但茂才公尚且不知,我还有什么好办法呢。

蓝译本:For this I am heartily ashamed of myself, but as the problem **defeated** even the younger Zhao, I fear I have no better option.

杨译本:This approximates to blindly following the *New Youth* magazine, and I am thoroughly ashamed of myself; but since even such a learned man as Mr. Chao's son could **not** solve my problem, what else can I do?

(3)表否定意义的形容词

原文:我所聊以自慰的,是还有一个"阿"字非常正确,绝无附会假借的缺点,颇可以就正于通人。

蓝译本:My only consolation in this whole sorry business is that one syllable of his name at least – "Ah" – can boast of an **unimpugnable** correctness.

杨译本:The only thing that consoles me is the fact that the character "Ah" is absolutely correct. This is definitely **not** the result of false analogy, and is well able to stand the test of scholarly criticism.

原文:即使与古人所撰《书法正传》的"正传"字面上很相混,也顾不得了。

蓝译本：Any similarity between the present work and the unforgettable *Real Story of Calligraphy*, by Mr Feng Wu of the Qing dynasty, is entirely **unintentional**.

杨译本：…and if this is reminiscent of the True Story of Calligraphy of the ancients, it can**not** be helped.

（4）表否定意义的词组

原文：赵太太还怕他因为春天的条件<u>不</u>敢来，而赵太爷以为不足虑：因为这是"我"去叫他的。

蓝译本：Mrs Zhao expressed concern that Ah-Q was **too** frightened **to** come, because of the events of last spring. Mr Zhao batted her worries away: this time, he had personally commanded Ah-Q's presence.

杨译本：Mrs. Chao was afraid that Ah Q dared **not** come because of the terms agreed upon that spring, but Mr. Chao did nor think this anything to worry about, because, as he said, "This time I sent for him."

本章小结

本章统计分析了 5 对译本总体副词特征，聚焦 3 类副词：程度副词、方式副词和否定副词。统计发现，母语译者使用的副词数量与种类平均高于非母语译者。（1）程度副词：非母语译者更多使用程度副词。统计译本中常见程度副词 very 和 so 后发现，非母语译者更偏爱使用这两个高频程度副词。比较鲁迅小说中最高频程度副词"非常"和"极"在蓝译本与杨译本中的翻译后发现，杨译本更多使用对等的程度副词，而蓝译本翻译手段更为丰富灵活。（2）方式副词：统计发现，平均而言，母语译者较非母语译者使用的方式副词种类更为丰富。（3）否定副词：非母语译者更多使用否定副词 not 及其缩写形式 n't，这说明母语译者使用了更多不含否定副词的否定意义表达。

第七章 代词使用对比

代词是指代名词或话语的一种词类,大多数代词具有名词和形容词的功能。英语中的代词,按其意义、特征及在句中的作用可分为:人称代词、物主代词、指示代词、反身代词、相互代词、疑问代词、关系代词、连接代词、不定代词和替代词 10 种。本章聚焦两类代词,即反身代词与指示代词。

一、反身代词

反身代词是一种表示反身或强调的代词,其基本作用是指代主语,使施动者把动作在形式上反射到施动者自己。5 对译本反身代词数据统计如下:

表 7.1 5 对译本反身代词数据统计

原作	鲁迅小说		《红楼梦》		《聊斋志异》		《骆驼祥子》		《浮生六记》	
译本	蓝译本	杨译本	霍译本	杨译本	闵译本	大中华译本	葛译本	施译本	拜伦译本	林译本
反身代词	271	225	166	100	218	111	226	302	67	72

上表显示,鲁迅小说、《红楼梦》《聊斋志异》3 对译本中,母语译者反身单词使用数量高于非母语译者,《骆驼祥子》与《浮生六记》情况相反。总体来看,母语译者更倾向于使用反身代词。

(一)反身代词概念及其功能

俞燕君(2016)将反身代词的功能划分为强调功能、照应功能和类指功能 3 种,并认为汉语的反身代词"自己"兼具这 3 种功能,而英语的反身代词仅有前 2 种功能。另外,就反身代词在句子中的语法成分而言,汉语反身代词"自己"分布极为自由,几乎可以出现在汉语名词短语能够出现的所有位置,包括主语、宾语、同位语、主语补足语、定语等。但英语反身代词受到的限制相对严格一些,如不可出现在时态句的主语、名词短语的定语位置,也无法受到定语修饰。

以上论述主要从汉语视角出发,对英汉反身代词的概念区别及其背后的思维方式差异的讨论不够彻底。贾光茂(2020)对英汉反身代词的概念基础进行了对比,指出英语反身代词有提示自我概念中主体和客体可以分离的功能,而汉语没有形成专门用来表达主客二分概念的反身构式。

张道真(2002)总结了英语反身代词的两种主要功能:① 反身功能,即作宾语,表示动作的承受者;② 强调功能,即用来对前面的名词或代词加以强调。辛克莱(2007)也归纳了反身代词的两个用法:① 作动词与介词的宾语,这时受行动影响的人或物与做出行动的人或物相同;② 反身代词也可以置于名词或者代词后表示强调。同样,剑桥语法区分了英语反身代词的4种功能:表达主宾一致、强调、与by搭配表独自和表礼貌。薄冰(2000)从反身代词在句中扮演的语法成分视角出发,将英语反身代词归纳为6种:① 用作及物动词的宾语;② 用作介词的宾语;③ 用作同位语;④ 用作表语;⑤(口语中)用作主语;⑥ 用于独立结构。

综合而言,与汉语相比,英语反身代词最显著的特征是其反身功能。虽然两种语言中的反身代词均可作为宾语,表达主宾一致,但其所呈现的形式和程度有所不同。英语反身代词的这一特点在动词的分类中得到印证。英语动词中专有一类名为反身动词(reflexive verb),即通常与反身代词连用的及物动词。(Sinclair,1991)

(二)鲁迅小说蓝译本与杨译本反身代词使用对比

这一思维上的差异,或许在汉语小说英译中有所反映。我们对鲁迅小说蓝译本与杨译本中的himself在句中的语法功能进行梳理统计,按照功能划分为两类:一类为反身功能型反身代词;另一类是强调功能型反身代词。

1. 反身功能型反身代词

此类反身代词大致有两种情况:一是反身代词作宾语;二是反身代词作介词宾语。作为宾语的结构为及物动词+himself。例如:

原文：这在阿Q，或者以为因为他是赵太爷的父亲，而其实也不然。

蓝译本：Ah-Q may have **deluded himself** into thinking it was because he actually was Mr Zhao's father; the real reason was very different.

作为介词宾语的结构为不及物动词＋介词＋himself。例如：

原文：而阿Q在精神上独不表格外的崇奉，他想：我的儿子会阔得多啦！

蓝译本：Only Ah-Q remained invulnerable to the glamour of their future promise: My son will be much richer than them! he **thought to himself**.

2. 强调功能型反身代词

此类反身代词也有若干种情形。

（1）作为同位语的结构为 **sb./he himself**。例如：

原文：而阿Q自己也不说，独有和别人口角的时候，间或瞪着眼睛道："我们先前——比你阔的多啦！你算是什么东西！"

蓝译本：Neither was **Ah-Q himself** particularly forthcoming on the subject, except when he got into arguments, viz.: "My ancestors were much richer than yours! Scum!"

（2）作为表语的结构为 be 动词＋**himself**。例如：

原文：打完之后，便心平气和起来，似乎打的是自己，被打的是别一个自己……

蓝译本：After this slapping his heart felt lighter, for it seemed as if the one who had given the slap was **himself**, the one slapped some other self…

我们将鲁迅小说两译本中的反身代词按照上述分类统计，数据如下表所示：

表7.2 鲁迅小说蓝译本与杨译本反身代词使用统计

功能	语法成分	蓝译本		杨译本	
		数量	种类	数量	种类
反身功能	宾语	46	33	25	24
	介词宾语	23	14	17	12
强调功能	同位语	24	/	20	/
	表语	0	/	2	/
合计		93	47	64	36

从上表数据可以看出,蓝译本共使用反身代词 himself 93 个,较杨译本多出 29 个。其中,作为宾语的 himself,在蓝译本中有 33 种,共 46 个,杨译本中 24 种,共 25 个。具体涉及动词如下。

(1)反身功能型反身代词——宾语

蓝译本(33/46):take himself to(2);take himself off(1);tell himself(1);delude himself(1);brace himself(1);propel himself(1);find himself(8);haul himself(1);hurl himself(2);recover himself(1);kick himself(1);call himself(1);compose himself(1);convince himself(1);calm himself(1);apply himself(3);consider himself(1);force himself(1);keep himself(1);lose himself(1);get himself(1);drag himself(2);park himself down(1);resign himself to(1);congratulate himself on(1);lose himself in(1);cough himself to sleep(1);heave himself to his feet(1);protect himself(1);extricate himself(1);prostrate himself(2);commit himself(1);declare himself(1)

杨译本(24/25):content himself(1);consider himself(1);brace himself(1);show himself(1);prove himself(1);contain himself(2);find himself(2);pick up himself(1);regard himself(1);consider himself(1);feel himself(1);concern himself with(1);express himself(1);support himself(1);drag himself(1);hang himself(1);reconcile himself to…(1);express himself(1);cough himself to sleep himself(1);correct himself himself(1);prostrate himself(2);let himself(1);commit himself to(1);better himself(1)

作为介词宾语的 himself,在蓝译本中有 14 种,共 23 个,杨译本中 12 种,共 17 个。具体如下。

(2)反身功能型反身代词——介词宾语

蓝译本(14/23):think to himself(7);fulminate to himself(1);feel pleased with himself(1);be in delight with himself(1);mutter to himself(3);muse to himself(1);wonder to himself(1);admit to himself(1);keep… to himself（1）; sigh to himself（1）; count sth. for himself（1）; look pleased with himself（1）; keep his teeth to himself（1）; make trouble for himself（1）

杨译本（12/17）: have a...opinion of himself（1）; think to himself（4）; say to himself（3）; make a name for himself（1）; give news of himself（1）; fry rice for himself（1）; choose for himself（1）; swear to himself（1）; say a word for himself（1）; count sth. for himself（1）; talk to himself（1）; come to himself（1）

不难看出，两译本统计数据在 himself 作为宾语成分时悬殊最大，即母语译者相比而言，更倾向于使用反身代词的反身功能，这与英汉两种语言中反身代词的差异相契合。

二、指示代词

指示代词（demonstrative pronoun）是表示指示概念的代词，用来指示或标识人和事物。与定冠词和人称代词一样，指示代词具有指定的含义，起指示作用，或代替前面已提到过的名词。指示代词有：this，that，these，those，such，same，it。薄冰（2000）归纳了指示代词的6种用法：用作主语、用作宾语、用作表语、用作定语、用作状语，为了强调而重复前面所讲的事情（多用于省略句和"主+系+表"结构）。

我们对5对译本中的指示代词进行统计，数据如下表所示。

表7.3 各译本指示代词使用统计对比

代词	鲁迅小说		《红楼梦》		《聊斋志异》		《骆驼祥子》		《浮生六记》	
	蓝译本	杨译本	霍译本	杨译本	闵译本	大中华译本	葛译本	施译本	拜伦译本	林译本
this	286	<u>534</u>	341	319	<u>310</u>	183	264	<u>383</u>	156	<u>218</u>
that	606	<u>858</u>	819	488	<u>559</u>	501	<u>969</u>	682	<u>407</u>	399
these	29	<u>82</u>	63	59	<u>31</u>	13	48	<u>73</u>	27	<u>38</u>
those	67	<u>93</u>	<u>48</u>	28	8	<u>21</u>	65	<u>69</u>	13	13
合计	988	<u>1567</u>	<u>1271</u>	894	<u>908</u>	718	<u>1346</u>	1207	603	<u>668</u>

上表显示，《红楼梦》《聊斋志异》《骆驼祥子》3 对译本中，母语译者指示代词使用数量高于非母语译者，鲁迅小说与《浮生六记》情况相反。

本研究将研究对象限于定语形式的指示代词,统计数据如下:

表7.4 各译本作为定语的指示代词使用对比

表达	鲁迅小说		《红楼梦》		《聊斋志异》		《骆驼祥子》		《浮生六记》	
	蓝译本	杨译本	霍译本	杨译本	闵译本	大中华译本	葛译本	施译本	拜伦译本	林译本
this+N	129	208	153	127	128	72	105	169	67	96
that+N	105	143	110	80	70	47	120	90	70	52
these+N	15	40	35	35	22	7	32	44	18	17
those+N	15	24	21	12	4	6	20	19	2	1
this+ADJ+N	40	45	27	17	38	11	19	35	3	5
that+ADJ+N	29	35	21	16	19	5	20	19	12	3
these+ADJ+N	0	8	7	2	1	1	3	4	2	1
those+ADJ+N	8	9	10	3	1	1	9	8	2	0
合计	341	512	384	292	283	150	328	388	176	175

本研究重点关注指示代词用法中所表达的情感色彩。指示代词 this(these)与 that(those)表感情色彩大致有3种情况:① this(these)/that(those)+双重属格,如 I don't like these novels of his;② this(these)/that(those)+隐喻结构,如 that pig of a husband;③ this(these)/that(those)+形容词(可选)+名词,如 He was one of those people who take delight in conveying disagreeable news. 鲁迅小说中蓝译本与杨译本有关上述3种表达的统计数据如下:

表7.5 鲁迅小说蓝译本与杨译本3类特殊指示代词表达结构统计

表达类型	蓝译本	杨译本
this(these)/that(those)+双重属格	16	1
this(these)/that(those)+隐喻结构	3	0
this(these)/that(those)+形容词(可选)+名词(指人)	46	36
合计	65	37

从上表数据可看出,在这3类特殊指示代词表达结构中,蓝译本数量均高于

杨译本。下面我们看看具体译例。

1. this(these)/that(those)+双重属格译例

原文：总而言之，这一篇也便是"本传"，但从我的文章着想，因为文体卑下，是"引车卖浆者流"所用的话，所以不敢僭称……

蓝译本：**This effort of mine**, I can only conclude, is the standard, official biography of the man; and yet the debased vulgarity of its content and characters causes me to shy, appalled, from such presumption.

杨译本：In short, this is really a "life", but since I write in vulgar vein using the language of hucksters and pedlars, I dare not presume to give it so high-sounding a title.

蓝译本中，this effort of mine 暗示给阿Q写传不是什么高尚的事业。

原文：然而这意见总反而在他脑里生长起来。

蓝译本：And yet – and yet, **this new philosophy of his** took ever deeper root in his mind.

杨译本：None the less, this viewpoint grew on him.

蓝译本中，This new philosophy of his 表明作者对主人公方玄绰"差不多"理念不以为然。

原文：他如果能懂事，早就点了灯笼火把，寻了那孝女来了。

蓝译本：If he was, he'd have skipped dinner to go and fetch **that girl of yours** back home.

杨译本：If he had any sense, he'd long since have lit a lantern or a torch and gone out to fetch that filial daughter.

原文中"那孝女"这一说法本身便不十分尊敬。蓝译本译为 that girl of yours，并用了 fetch 动词，意味更浓。杨译本也用了指示代词 that。

原文：他们的第一大问题是，在怎样对付这"承重孙"……

蓝译本：The principal obstacle to be anticipated was **this chief mourner of hers**…

杨译本：But the immediate problem was how to cope with this grandson.

蓝译本和杨译本均使用了指示代词 this，蓝译本使用了双重属格，更为着重。

原文：他连喝两口酒，默默地想着，突然，仰起脸来看着我问道，"你在图谋的职业也还是毫无把握罢？"

蓝译本：He took another couple of gulps and sat in silence, thinking. Suddenly, he looked back up at me. "Still no news about **that job of yours**?"

杨译本：He took two sips of liquor in succession, then fell silent. Suddenly, looking up, he asked, "I suppose you have had no luck either in finding work?"

蓝译本中 That job of yours 言语轻视，符合原文语气。

原文：十三大人还疑心我们得了什么好处。有什么屁好处呢？

蓝译本：**That cousin of his** was convinced he'd given the loot to us, but we didn't get a damn thing.

杨译本：His cousin still suspects we got something out of him. Heaven knows, we got nothing.

原文中对十三大人的疑心颇不以为然，故蓝译本的 that cousin of his 语气恰当。

原文：杨二嫂发现了这件事，自己很以为功，便拿了那狗气杀，飞也似的跑了……

蓝译本：Exceptionally pleased with **this discovery of hers**, she flew out of the door, scooping up en route a wooden trough…

杨译本：After making this discovery Mrs. Yang was very pleased with herself, and flew off raking the dog-teaser with her.

原文中"自己很以为功"是人物内心活动，译为 this discovery of hers，再现了叙述者的态度。

原文：你想，"小畜生"姘上了小寡妇，就不要我，事情有这么容易的？

蓝译本：**That pig of a husband of mine** jumped into bed with that young widow, then threw me out of my own home – think I should just lie down and take it?

杨译本：Just think! Young Beast carried on with that little widow and decided he didn't want me. But is it as simple as that?

原文中"小畜生"分明是贬义表达，除了将畜生译为 pig，译者还使用了指示代词的双重属格结构加强了这一语气。

原文："老畜生"只知道帮儿子，也不要我，好容易呀！

蓝译本：Then **that pig of a father of his**'ll play any tune his son tells him to.

杨译本：Old Beast just egged on his son and tried to get rid of me too—as if it were all that easy!

本例与上例旨趣相当，只是"小畜生"换成了"老畜生"。

原文：他单觉得这屋子太静，太大，太空罢了。

蓝译本：All she knew was that this room was too silent, too large, too empty.

杨译本：Only that <u>**this room of hers**</u> was too quiet, too big, too empty.

杨译本中，双重属格结构的使用起到了加强语气的作用。

原文：——你那，什么呢，你的朋友罢，子君，你可知道，她死了。

蓝译本：By the way, that—<u>**that friend of yours**</u>, Zijun. She's dead, you know.

杨译本：That—er—<u>that friend of yours</u>, Tzu-chun, I suppose you know, is dead.

原文中"你的朋友"是加强语气，双重属格较为贴近。杨译本也使用了这一结构。

原文：这位N先生本来脾气有点夸张，时常生些无谓的气，说些不通世故的话。

蓝译本：Now <u>**this Mr. N of mine**</u> was famed for the eccentricities of his mood: for his habit of flying into inexplicable tempers, or coming out with views some way out of step with conventional wisdom.

杨译本：This Mr. N is rather irascible. He often loses his temper for no reason and makes tactless remarks.

原文中"这位先生"脾气夸张，无谓生气，不通世故，译为 this Mr. N of mine 语气刚好。

原文：包好，包好！这样的趁热吃下。这样的人血馒头，什么痨病都包好！

蓝译本：Guaranteed! Eat it hot. **That consumption of his** won't stand a chance, not against a bun dipped in human blood!

杨译本：A guaranteed cure! Eaten warm like this. A roll dipped in human blood like this can cure any consumption!

蓝译本中的双重属格作强调，应和"什么痨病都包好"的语气。

原文："包好，包好！"康大叔瞥了小栓一眼，仍然回过脸，对众人说，"夏三爷真是乖角儿，要是他不先告官，连他满门抄斩。"

蓝译本："Guaranteed!" Mr Kang glanced at the boy, before turning back to his audience. "Sharp as a tack, **that uncle of his**. If he hadn't informed when he did, the authorities would have gone for the whole family – root and branch."

杨译本："A guaranteed cure! Kang glanced at the child, then turned back to address the company."Third Uncle Hsia is really smart. If he hadn't informed, even his family would have been executed, and their property confiscated.

原文中说夏三爷是"乖角儿"译为 this uncle of his，更贴近这一语气。

原文：我先是诧异，接着是很不安，似乎这话于我有关系。

蓝译本：I was first bewildered, then uneasy, as if **this throwaway comment of his** was in some way connected to me.

杨译本：At first I felt astonished, then very uncomfortable, thinking these words must refer to me.

"这话"不是好话，形容词 throwaway 加上双重属格结构较为符合人物心理。

原文：后来大家又都知道了她的脾气，只要有孩子在眼前，便似笑非笑的先问她，道："祥林嫂，你们的阿毛如果还在，不是也就有这么大了么？"

蓝译本：In time, everyone learnt to tease her about **this new trick of hers**. "If your Ah-mao were still alive," they would ask, trying not to smirk, whenever a child happened to be in sight, "wouldn't he be about as big as that?"

杨译本：Later everybody knew what she was like, and it only needed a child present for them to ask her with an artificial smile, "Hsiang Lin's Wife, if your Ah Mao were alive, wouldn't he be just as big as that?"

原文中描绘的可怜人祥林嫂是个十足的悲剧人物，不断叨扰人，不讨人喜欢，作者也不耐烦，蓝译本中 this new trick of hers 符合这一语气。

2. this(these)/that(those)＋隐喻结构译例

原文：就专凭他们"老畜生""小畜生"摆布；他们会报丧似的急急忙忙钻狗洞，巴结人……

蓝译本：**That pig of a husband** and **pig of a father-in-law** have pulled everyone's strings, they'll stoop at nothing, scraping and bowing…

杨译本：He let Old Beast and Young Beast have their way in everything. They stoop to every means, however foul, to fawn on those above them…

原文中，"老畜生"和"小畜生"都是贬义的说法，蓝译本用指示代词＋隐喻结构表达这一语气。

原文：那"小畜生"不分青红皂白，就夹脸一嘴巴……

蓝译本：But I still got slapped, round both sides of my face, by **that stupid pig of a husband**.

杨译本：But that Young Beast wouldn't distinguish black from white. He gave me a slap on the cheek…

此例与上例一样，"小畜生"被译为指示代词隐喻结构。

原文：而小尼姑并不然，这也足见异端之可恶。

蓝译本：**That heretic vixen of a nun**, with her shameless naked face.

杨译本：The little nun had not covered her face, however, and this is another proof of the odiousness of the heretic.

蓝译本将"小尼姑"比作 vixen，赋予其较强的情感色彩。

3. this(these)/that(those)＋形容词(可选)＋名词

指示代词 this(these)/that(those)＋形容词(可选)＋名词的结构，也常用来强调某种情感和态度。我们对在蓝译本与杨译本中的此类表达进行统计，数据如下表所示。

表达	蓝译本（46）	杨译本（36）
this(these) / that(those) + 名词	this oracle; that scum; that heretic; this bastard; this bastard; that rebellion; this deputy; that publisher; that Sevenpounder; that girl; that girl; that girl; this grandmother; that Daoist; that Lianshu; that cousin; this zha; this Mrs Yang; that Shuisheng; that woman; this brother; that pig; that pig; that widow; this Mrs Guang; that weasel; that pig; that whore; this man; that Zijun; that friend; this Mr. N; this couple; this family; that uncle; that boy; that crow （37）	that woman; this dog; that man; this man; that priest; this man; that Sevenpounder; this grandmother; this grandson; this grandmother; this grandmother; this boy; that dog; that woman; that woman; this uncle; that bitch; that whore; this man; that friend; that supervisor; this couple; this man; that crow; this conjuror; this fellow （26）
this(these) / that(those) + 形容词 + 名词	this utter weed; this chief mourner; that old man; that young widow; that old fool; that stupid pig; that wicked whore; that squeaky runt; that old man （9）	this little widow; this little widow; that filial daughter; that filial daughter; that small hero; this old man; that little widow; that Young Beast; that Old Chuan; that young rogue （10）

上表统计了两类表达：一种为 this(these) / that(those) + 名词结构；第二种为 this(these) / that(those) + 形容词 + 名词。前一种结构，蓝译本为 36 项，较杨译本 26 项多出 10 项，第二种结构杨译本较蓝译本多出 1 例。蓝译本总数较杨译本多出 10 例。

本章小结

本章对比了母语译者译本与非母语译者译本对代词的使用，重点考察反身代词与指示代词的使用。对比发现：母语译者译本更倾向于使用更多表达反身功能的反身代词以及更多指示代词；对比鲁迅小说的蓝译本与杨译本后发现，蓝译本更偏好使用表情感的特定代词短语表达。

第八章 情态动词使用对比

情态动词（modal verb）是表示语气的词语，但其不能独立作谓语，只能和动词原形一起构成谓语。情态动词用于行为动词前，表说话人对动作或状态的看法或主观设想。情态动词虽然数量不多，但用途广泛，常见的有：can(could)，may（might），must，need，ought to，dare(dared)，shall(should)，will(would)，have to。

在本章中，我们对情态动词的研究聚焦以下两点：（1）母语译者与非母语译者在情态动词使用的数量和类别上的差异；（2）二者在情态动词使用上所表现出的其他质性差异。

一、情态动词总体对比

我们先将母语译者与非母语译者情态动词使用情况进行整体对比、分析，统计数据如下：

表 8.1 母语译者与非母语译者情态动词使用统计对比

情态动词	母语译者						非母语译者					
	总数	百分比	肯定	省略式	否定	省略式	总数	百分比	肯定	省略式	否定	省略式
will	450	10.00%	427	5	23	2	643	12.80%	575	181	91	68
would	1204	26.76%	1125	1	79	2	1353	26.93%	1221	44	132	53
can	469	10.42%	412	\	57	0	522	10.39%	379	\	143	97
could	1028	22.85%	850	0	178	4	1052	20.94%	813	0	239	62
may	73	1.62%	63	\	10	0	111	2.21%	109	\	2	0

（续表）

情态动词	母语译者						非母语译者					
	总数	百分比	肯定	省略式	否定	省略式	总数	百分比	肯定	省略式	否定	省略式
might	202	4.49%	188	/	14	0	188	3.74%	181	/	7	1
shall	67	1.49%	67	/	0	0	85	1.69%	84	/	1	0
should	307	6.82%	290	0	17	2	320	6.37%	283	12	37	18
ought	42	0.93%	37	/	5	0	29	0.58%	14	/	15	0
need	2	0.04%	2	/	0	0	10	0.20%	6	/	4	1
must	286	6.36%	283	/	3	0	354	7.04%	340	/	14	7
have to	369	8.20%	363	/	6	0	358	7.12%	343	/	15	10
合计	4499		4107	6	392	10	5025		4348	237	700	317

我们基于上表数据一一分析母语译者与非母语译者情态动词使用差异。

（一）数量与种类对比

从总体数量上看，母语译者使用了 4499 个情态动词，非母语译者则使用了 5025 个，二者相差 526 个，种类相同，表明非母语译者总体上更倾向于使用情态动词。

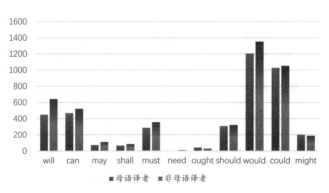

图 8.1 母语—非母语译者情态动词使用数据对比

(二)省略形式对比

母语译者使用了省略形式的情态动词共计16个,而非母语译者则使用了554个,压倒性地高于母语译者。从某种程度上,这一数据对比反映了母语译者的词汇语域正式度高于非母语译者。请看下面的数据对比。

表8.2 母语—非母语译者情态动词省略形式使用对比

序号	形态	情态动词	母语译者	非母语译者
1	肯定形式	'll	5	181
2		'd(would)	1	44
3		'd(should)	0	15
4	否定形式	can't	0	97
5		won't	2	68
6		couldn't	4	62
7		wouldn't	2	53
8		shouldn't	2	18
9		mightn't	0	1
10		needn't	0	1
11		mustn't	0	7
	合计		16	547

从上表数据看,母语译者共使用16个省略形式:'ll 5例,'d(would)1例,won't 2例,couldn't 4例,shouldn't 2例,wouldn't 2例。相比之下,非母语译者则使用了547个省略形式,'d(would)44例,'d(should)15例,can't 97例,won't 68例,couldn't 62例,wouldn't 53例,shouldn't 18例,mightn't 1例,needn't 1例,mustn't 7例。

缩写形式是非正式文体的指标之一。这一数据对比从侧面证明,汉语小说英译中的母语译者更偏向使用正式文体。

(三)否定形式对比

母语译者使用情态动词否定形式 386 个，非母语译者使用情态动词否定形式 685 个，大大高于母语译者，表明非母语译者相对而言更多使用情态动词的否定形式。我们对母语译者与非母语译者情态动词否定形式使用情况进行统计，数据如下表所示。

表 8.3 母语—非母语译者情态动词否定形式对比统计

序号	情态动词	母语译者	非母语译者
1	will	23	91
2	would	79	132
3	can	57	143
4	could	178	239
5	may	10	2
6	might	14	7
7	shall	0	1
8	should	17	37
9	ought	5	15
10	need	0	4
11	must	3	14
总计		386	685

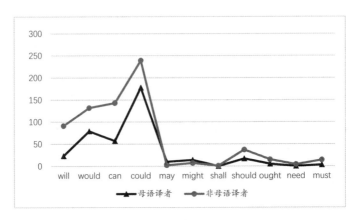

图 8.2 母语 – 非母语译者情态动词否定式统计对比

二、鲁迅小说蓝译本与杨译本情态动词使用对比分析

我们聚焦鲁迅小说的蓝译本与杨译本，对比两个译本在情态动词使用方面的差异。两译本数据统计如下：

表 8.4 鲁迅小说蓝译本与杨译本情态动词使用对比

情态动词	蓝译本						杨译本					
	总数	比例	肯定	肯定省略式	否定	否定省略式	总数	比例	肯定	肯定省略式	否定	否定省略式
can	78	9.19%	75	/	3	0	148	10.29%	94	/	61	54
could	160	18.85%	147	/	13	4	325	22.60%	228	/	97	31
may	16	1.88%	14	/	2	/	38	2.64%	38	/	0	/
might	45	5.30%	41	/	4	0	42	2.92%	42	/	0	0
must	69	8.13%	69	/	0	0	141	9.81%	132	/	9	4
ought	4	0.47%	4	/	0	/	9	0.63%	9	/	0	/
shall	2	0.24%	2	/	0	0	25	1.74%	25	/	0	0
should	52	6.12%	50	0	2	2	77	5.35%	69	1	8	6
will	83	9.78%	78	5	5	2	170	11.82%	136	51	34	27
would	278	32.74%	268	1	10	1	368	25.59%	325	9	43	23
need	0	0.00%	0	/	0	0	4	0.28%	3	/	1	0
have to	62	7.30%	62	/	0	0	91	6.33%	86	/	5	2
合计	849	100%	810	6	39	9	1438	100%	1187	61	258	147

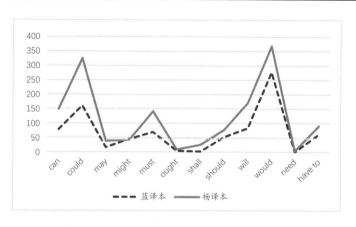

图 8.3 鲁迅小说蓝译本与杨译本情态动词使用统计对比

从上述数据对比，我们可以得出以下几点结论：

（1）蓝译本与杨译本的情态动词使用倾向符合母语译者与非母语译者对比特征。蓝译本共使用849个情态动词，而杨译本使用了1438个，远远高于蓝译本。

（2）杨译本更偏向使用与否定副词not组成的否定态，共使用了258个，远高于蓝译本的39个。这一点也符合母语译者与非母语译者整体对比情况。

（3）杨译本使用更多省略形式的情态动词，其中肯定形式有61例，否定形式147例；而蓝译本仅仅使用了15例，不到前者的1/10。

综上所述，蓝译本和杨译本各项数据统计均符合比较典型的母语译者与非母语译者的文体倾向。

（一）鲁迅小说情态动词"应该"英译对比

上表显示非母语译者倾向于使用情态动词，数量高于母语译者。为了进一步深入分析，我们以鲁迅小说中的情态动词"应该"为例，比较两译本在处理该词时的差异，以窥一斑。我们在蓝译本与杨译本中检索词汇"应该"，提取出所有译例做统计分析。经统计，汉语情态动词"应该"在两译本中共有以下两类情况：（1）情态动词，如should，must，had to，ought to，need to等；（2）非情态动词结构，意译为其他结构。具体统计如下：

表8.5 鲁迅小说蓝译本与杨译本"应该"英译对比

情态动词	蓝译本	杨译本
should	7	14
ought to	1	5
must	1	1
have to	1	1
would	3	3
can	1	0
need	1	0
小结	15	24
去情态化	18	10
合计	33	33

从上述统计可以看出：(1) 蓝译本使用了 7 类共计 15 个情态动词对应原文的"应该"，而杨译本使用了 5 类共计 24 个。从数量上而言，蓝译本更少使用情态动词，但从类别上来看，蓝译本的情态动词更加多样；(2) 杨译本使用了 14 个 should，对应原文"应该"，蓝译本仅 7 例，这从另一个视角印证了杨译本翻译策略偏向直译，蓝译本更加灵活；(3) 蓝译本中有 18 个译例使用了非情态动词的谓语结构，大大高于杨译本的 10 例，这也说明了与杨译本相比，蓝译本更不拘泥于原文。这一数据呼应了上文的统计发现，即非母语译者使用更多情态动词。

全部译例如下：

(1) 蓝译本 should（7 例）

原文：他飘飘然的飞了大半天，飘进土谷祠，照例**应该**躺下便打鼾。

蓝译本：Eventually, he floated off to the Temple of Earth and Grain, where, according to well-established custom, he **should** have immediately lain down and began snoring.

原文：他们想而又想，才想出静修庵里有一块"皇帝万岁万万岁"的龙牌，是**应该**赶紧革掉的……

蓝译本：After giving the matter some further thought, they remembered there was a tablet in the Convent of Quiet Cultivation wishing the emperor "Ten thousand thousand thousand thousand years of life" Deciding, quite naturally, that this **should** be the first thing to go…

原文：而阿 Q 总觉得自己太失意：既然革了命，不**应该**只是这样的。

蓝译本：But Ah-Q was nagged by a sense of frustration: that things **should** be different, now there had been a revolution.

原文：我不去！这是官俸，不是赏钱，照例**应该**由会计科送来的。

蓝译本：No! It's not a bonus – it's my regular salary. Payroll **should** just send it out like they always do.

原文：吓，什么学堂，造就了些什么？我简直说：**应该**统统关掉！

蓝译本：A big fat waste of time, that's what these schools are. Shut the lot of them down – that's what they **should** do.

原文：常说家庭<u>应该</u>破坏，一领薪水却一定立即寄给他的祖母，一日也不拖延。

蓝译本：He was always declaring that the family **should** be abolished, and yet every month he'd send his salary back to his grandmother as soon as he got it.

原文：我<u>不应该</u>将真实说给子君，我们相爱过，我应该永久奉献她我的说谎。

蓝译本：I **shouldn't** have told her the truth. For the sake of the love we had once shared, I should have smiled and told her lies for ever.

（2）杨译本 should（14 例）

原文：孔子曰，"名不正则言不顺"。这原是<u>应该</u>极注意的。

杨译本：Confucius said, "If the name is not correct, the words will not ring true"; and this axiom **should** be most scrupulously observed.

原文：他想：不错，<u>应该</u>有一个女人，断子绝孙便没有人供一碗饭……应该有一个女人。

杨译本：…and he thought, Quite right, I **should** take a wife; for if a man dies sonless he has no one to sacrifice a bowl of rice to his spirit … I ought to have a wife.

原文：赵太爷便在晚饭桌上，和秀才大爷讨论，以为阿Q实在有些古怪，我们门窗<u>应该</u>小心些。

杨译本：Mr. Chao discussed the matter that evening at dinner with his son, the successful county candidate, suggesting that there must be something queer about Ah Q, and that they **should** be more careful about their doors and windows.

原文：而阿Q总觉得自己太失意：既然革了命，<u>不应该</u>只是这样的。

杨译本：He thought since a revolution had taken place, it **should** involve more than this.

原文：本来对面是虽然受了三枝箭，<u>应该</u>都聚在一处的，因为箭箭相衔，不差丝发。

杨译本：They **should** have struck the moon in the same place, for they followed each other without a hair's breadth between them.

原文："我不去！这是官俸，不是赏钱，照例<u>应该</u>由会计科送来的。"

杨译本："Not I! My official stipent, not charity! By rights the accountant's office **should** send it over."

原文：常说家庭<u>应该</u>破坏，一领薪水却一定立即寄给他的祖母，一日也不拖延。

杨译本：And while maintaining that the family system **should** be abolished, he sent his salary to his grandmother the same day that he drew it.

原文："你<u>应该</u>将世间看得光明些。"我叹惜着说。

杨译本："You **should** take a more cheerful view." I sighed.

原文：如果没有门当户对的，先买几个姨太太也可以：人是总<u>应该</u>像个样子的。

杨译本：And if no suitable family could be found, at least he could have bought a few concubines to go on with. People **should** keep up appearances.

原文：他们<u>应该</u>有新的生活，为我们所未经生活过的。

杨译本：They **should** have a new life, a life we have never experienced.

原文：一种是以为从来如此，<u>应该</u>吃的。

杨译本：Some of them thought that since it had always been so, men **should** be eaten.

原文：我不<u>应该</u>将真实说给子君，我们相爱过，我应该永久奉献她我的说谎。

杨译本：I **shouldn't** have told Tzu-chun the truth. Since we had loved each other, I should have gone on lying to her.

原文：六一公公看见我，便停了楫，笑道，"请客？——这是<u>应该</u>的。"

杨译本：When the old man saw me, he stopped punting, and chuckled. "Treating a visitor? So you **should**."

原文：以及俯伏得有怎么低，<u>应该</u>采作国民的模范等等。

杨译本：…They had prostrated themselves so low that they **should** be considered as examples to all the nation!

（3）蓝译本 would（3例）

原文：赵太爷便在晚饭桌上，和秀才大爷讨论，以为阿Q实在有些古怪，我们门窗<u>应该</u>小心些。

蓝译本：On discussing the question at the dinner table with his learned son, Mr Zhao concluded that while the exercise of caution about the house **would** be advisable.

原文：叫他假洋鬼子固然是不行的了，洋人也不妥，革命党也不妥，或者就<u>应该</u>叫洋先生了罢。

蓝译本：Fake Foreign Devil didn't quite sound right any more; but neither did he think Foreigner or Revolutionary **would** do. Mr Foreigner, perhaps?

原文：豫计连殳的到来，<u>应该</u>已是入殓的时候了。

蓝译本：When Lianshu arrived, they calculated, it **would** be time to place the deceased in her coffin.

（4）杨译本 would（3例）

原文：叫他假洋鬼子固然是不行的了，洋人也不妥，革命党也不妥，或者就<u>应该</u>叫洋先生了罢。

杨译本：Obviously he could not call the man "Imitation Foreign Devil", and neither "Foreigne" nor "Revolutionary" seemed suitable. Perhaps the best form of address **would** be "Mr. Foreigner."

原文：豫计连殳的到来，<u>应该</u>已是入殓的时候了。

杨译本：…crowded the room anticipating Wei's return, which **would** be in time for the funeral.

原文：他飘飘然的飞了大半天，飘进土谷祠，照例<u>应该</u>躺下便打鼾。

杨译本：For quite a time he seemed to be flying, and he flew into the Tutelary God's Temple, where he **would** normally have snored as soon as he lay down.

（5）蓝译本 ought to（1例）

原文：他想：不错，<u>应该</u>有一个女人，断子绝孙便没有人供一碗饭。

蓝译本："She's quite right," he thought to himself. "I **ought to** have a woman. If I die without descendants, I'll have no one to offer a bowl of rice at my grave..."

（6）杨译本 ought to（5例）

原文：他们想而又想，才想出静修庵里有一块"皇帝万岁万万岁"的龙牌，是<u>应该</u>赶紧革掉的。

杨译本：After racking their brains for some time, they remembered that in the Convent of Quiet Self-improvement there was an imperial tablet inscribed "Long Live the Emperor" which **ought to** be done away with at once.

原文：搅乱天下的就是她们，<u>应该</u>很严的办一办。"

杨译本：…but these girls are the ones who turn everything upside down. They **ought to** be very severely dealt with indeed…

原文：记着！这些字<u>应该</u>记着。将来做掌柜的时候，写账要用。

杨译本：Mind you remember! You **ought to** remember such characters, because later when you have a shop of your own, you'll need them to make up your accounts.

原文：我觉得新的希望就只在我们的分离；她<u>应该</u>决然舍去。

杨译本：I felt that our only hope lay in parting. She **ought to** make a clean break.

原文：他是我的本家，比我长一辈，<u>应该</u>称之日"四叔"是，一个讲理学的老监生。

杨译本：He is a member of our clan, and belongs to the generation before mine, so I **ought to** call him "Fourth Uncle." An old student of the imperial college who went in for Neo-Confucianism...

（7）蓝译本 have to （1例）

原文：临末，因为在晚上，<u>应该</u>送地保加倍酒钱四百文。

蓝译本：As their meeting drew to its conclusion, Ah-Q **had to** tip the constable four hundred coppers—double the usual rate –because he'd been called out at night.

（8）杨译本 have to（1例）

原文：临末，因为在晚上，<u>应该</u>送地保加倍酒钱四百文。

杨译本：Finally, since it was night-time, Ah Q **had to** pay double and give the bailiff four hundred cash.

（9）蓝译本 need to（1例）

原文：搅乱天下的就是她们，<u>应该</u>很严的办一办。

蓝译本：It's the women who've brought the country to its knees. They **need** to be taught a lesson they won't forget.

（10）蓝译本 can（1例）

原文："……你<u>应该</u>将世间看得光明些。"我叹惜着说。

蓝译本："…**Can't** you try to see the bright side of things?"

（11）蓝译本 must（1例）

原文：我觉得新的希望就只在我们的分离；她<u>应该</u>决然舍去。

蓝译本：Fresh hope, I felt, lay only in our separation; she **must** resolve to give the whole thing up.

（12）杨译本 must（1例）

原文：就在前天，我在城里买了一口小棺材——因为我预料那地下的<u>应该</u>早已朽烂了。

杨译本：So the day before yesterday I bought a small coffin, because I reckoned that the one under the ground **must** have rotted long ago…

（13）蓝译本无情态动词（18例）

原文：孔子曰，"名不正则言不顺"。这原是<u>应该</u>极注意的。

蓝译本：As Confucius says: "If a name is not right, the words will not ring true." Wise words indeed.

原文：这飘飘然的精神，在礼教上是<u>不应该</u>有的……

蓝译本：What **abominable** creatures women truly were…

第八章　情态动词使用对比

原文：本来对面是虽然受了三枝箭，<u>应该</u>都聚在一处的，因为箭箭相衔，不差丝发。

蓝译本：As at one instant, the arrows whipped away from the bow, the action blurred with speed, their separate trajectories coalescing into a single hum.

原文：……他先恭维我不去索薪，不肯亲领，非常之清高，一个人正<u>应该</u>这样做。

蓝译本：… he told me how **well** he thought I'd **behaved** through the whole business, not asking for my salary, refusing to pick the cheque up myself, and so on and so forth.

原文：便赶紧改口说，"我也没有闹什么脾气，我不过教学程<u>应该</u>懂事些。"

蓝译本："I'm not picking on him," he quickly changed tack. "I'm just offering constructive criticism."

原文：我倒有一个在这里：《孝女行》。那是实事，<u>应该</u>表彰表彰她。我今天在大街上……

蓝译本：How about: The Filial Granddaughter. I got the idea from someone I saw in town today. A real role model.

原文：如果没有门当户对的，先买几个姨太太也可以：人是总<u>应该</u>像个样子的。

蓝译本：Or even if he couldn't get someone from a good family, he could have bought in a few concubines. Kept up appearances, at least.

原文：他们<u>应该</u>有新的生活，为我们所未经生活过的。

蓝译本：I wanted new, different lives for them, lives that we had not lived.

原文：记着！这些字<u>应该</u>记着。将来做掌柜的时候，写账要用。

蓝译本：Don't forget it! When you get to be manager of this place, you'll need it for your accounts.

原文：一种是以为从来如此，<u>应该</u>吃的……

蓝译本：Some believed that the eating of men must go on because it was how things had always been.

原文：去年木叔带了六位儿子去拆平了他家的灶，谁不说<u>应该</u>？

蓝译本：Everyone was right behind you when you and your six sons flattened his family's stove last year...

原文：我看见我是一个卑怯者，<u>应该</u>被摈于强有力的人们，无论是真实者，虚伪者。

蓝译本：What a coward I was: I **deserved** to be thrown aside by those who were stronger than me – whether they spoke the truth or lies.

原文：六一公公看见我，便停了楫，笑道，"请客？——这是<u>应该</u>的。"

蓝译本：Catching sight of me, Liu Yi rested his pole. "A guest?" he said, smiling. "Ah, excellent – excellent."

原文：这<u>应该</u>是真实的，但在我却未曾感得；我住得久了……

蓝译本：Though there was probably truth in what he said, I couldn't feel it myself. I'd lived here too many years.

原文：他是向来主张自食其力的，常说女人可以畜牧，男人就<u>应该</u>种田。

蓝译本：Practising self-sufficiency had always been another of his notions: women, he was often saying, could concentrate on the livestock, while their men worked the land.

原文：就在前天，我在城里买了一口小棺材——因为我豫料那地下的<u>应该</u>早已朽烂了。

蓝译本：The day before yesterday, I bought a little coffin in town, supposing the old one would be completely rotten by now.

原文：他是我的本家，比我长一辈，<u>应该</u>称之曰"四叔"是，一个讲理学的老监生。

蓝译本：As he was a distant relative of mine, the generation above me, I addressed him as Uncle. A diehard Neo-Confucian of the old Imperial College…

原文：<u>应该</u>有一个女人。

蓝译本：A woman's what I need.

（14）杨译本无情态动词（10例）

原文：这飘飘然的精神，在礼教上是<u>不应</u>该有的……

杨译本：Such light-headedness, according to the classical canons, is most **reprehensible**…

原文：他先恭维我不去索薪，不肯亲领，非常之清高，一个人正<u>应该</u>这样做。

杨译本：First he praised me for not going to demand payment and refusing to fetch my pay, calling me most high-minded, a **fine** example to others.

原文：吓，什么学堂，造就了些什么？我简直说：<u>应该</u>统统关掉！

杨译本：What use is such a school, I ask you? What I say is: Close the whole lot of them!

原文：便赶紧改口说，"我也没有闹什么脾气，我不过教学程<u>应该</u>懂事些。"

杨译本：He hastily changed his tune. "I'm not losing my temper. I'm just telling Hsueh-cheng to learn a little sense."

原文：我倒有一个在这里：孝女行。那是实事，<u>应该</u>表彰表彰她。我今天在大街上……

杨译本：I've thought of one. How about The Filial Daughter? It's a true story, and she **deserves** to be eulogized. On the main street today…

原文：去年木叔带了六位儿子去拆平了他家的灶，谁不说<u>应该</u>？

杨译本：When you took your six sons to tear down their kitchen range last year, who didn't say you were right?

原文：我看见我是一个卑怯者，<u>应该</u>被摈于强有力的人们，无论是真实者，虚伪者。

杨译本：I realized I was a weakling. I **deserved** to be cast out by the strong, no matter whether they were truthful or hypocritical.

原文：这<u>应该</u>是真实的，但在我却未曾感得；我住得久了。

杨译本：This was no doubt his honest feeling, but not mine: I was an old resident.

原文：他是向来主张自食其力的，常说女人可以畜牧，男人就<u>应该</u>种田。

杨译本：A great advocate of self-sufficiency, he was all in favor of women keeping livestock and of men tilling the land.

原文：以及俯伏得有怎么低，<u>应该</u>采作国民的模范等等……

杨译本：…the abjection of their prostrations, how richly they **deserved** the accolade of model subject…

（二）缩写形式对比

蓝译本与杨译本情态动词省略形式统计数据如下：

表8.6 鲁迅小说蓝译本与杨译本情态动词缩写形式对比

序号	形态	情态动词	蓝译本	杨译本
1	肯定形式	'll	5	51
2		'd（would）	1	9
3		'd（should）	0	1
4	否定形式	can't	0	54
5		won't	2	27
6		couldn't	4	31
7		wouldn't	1	23
8		shouldn't	2	6
9		mightn't	0	0
10		needn't	0	0
11		mustn't	0	2
	合计		15	204

从上表数据看，蓝译本共使用了15个省略形式：其中'll 5例，'d（would）1例，won't 2例，couldn't 4例，shouldn't 2例，wouldn't 1例。相比之下，杨译本则使用了204个省略形式：'ll 51例，'d（would）9例，'d（should）1例，can't 54例，

won't 27 例，couldn't 31 例，wouldn't 23 例，shouldn't 6 例，mustn't 2 例。这一数据对比从侧面证明，蓝译本的文体比杨译本更正式。

（三）否定形式对比

表 8.7 鲁迅小说蓝译本与杨译本情态动词否定形式对比

序号	情态动词	蓝译本	杨译本
1	can	3	61
2	could	13	97
3	may	2	0
4	might	4	0
5	must	0	9
6	ought	0	0
7	shall	0	0
8	should	2	8
9	will	5	34
10	would	10	43
11	need	0	1
12	have to	0	5
合计		39	258

从上表可以看出，蓝译本共使用了 39 例情态动词否定形式，而杨译本共使用了 258 例，远远高于前者。我们以 can 的否定形式为例，分析两译本为何有这样的差异。蓝译本共使用 3 例 can 的否定形式，杨译本为 61 例，比蓝译本多出 58 例。对于杨译本中情态动词 can 的否定形式，除了同样使用 can 的否定形式，蓝译本还采用了诸多变通的处理方法：其他情态动词否定形式；非情态动词否定形式；非动词否定形式；表否定意义的词汇；表肯定意义的词汇；其他形式的熟语。译例如下：

1. 使用 can 的否定形式

蓝译本中有 3 例 can 的否定形式，如下例。

原文："我……我……不认得字。"阿 Q 一把抓住了笔，惶恐而且惭愧的说。

蓝译本："I ...I ... <u>can't</u> write,"Ah-Q confessed–ashamed, afraid–grasping the brush.

杨译本："I—I—<u>can't</u> write," said Ah Q, shamefaced, nervously holding the brush.

2. 其他情态动词否定形式

在某些译例中，蓝译本使用其他情态动词的否定形式，如 will 和 would 的否定形式。

原文：但这些话你只可以哄哄老婆子，本人面前捣什么鬼？俺向来就只是打猎，没有弄过你似的剪径的玩艺儿……

蓝译本：You might be able to humbug old women, but you **won't** fool me! I'm a hunter, not a highway robber – unlike some people round here.

杨译本：Maybe you can impress old women that way, but you **can't** impose on me. I've always stuck to hunting, never taken to highway robbery like you…

3. 非情态动词的否定形式

非情态动词的否定形式也是蓝译本的应对策略之一，如下例。

原文："阿……Q 哥，像我们这样穷朋友是<u>不要紧的</u>……"赵白眼慌慌的说，似乎想探革命党的口风。

蓝译本："Ah—...I mean, Q, my friend, I shouldn't waste your time on people like us, " Zhao Baiyan nervously ventured. "People like us –we **haven't** a bean, you know."

杨译本："Ah—Q, old man, poor friends of yours like us **can't** possibly matter…" said Chao Pai-yen apprehensively, as if sounding out the revolutionaries' attitude.

4. 非动词否定形式

一些否定形式不涉及动词，如下例。

原文：他说："这不能。须大雪下了才好。我们沙地上，下了雪，我扫出一块空地来，用短棒支起一个大竹匾，撒下秕谷，看鸟雀来吃时……"

蓝译本："<u>Not today</u>. It's best when there's been snow. Then you clear a patch of sand, prop a basket on a short stick and scatter some blighted grain."

杨译本："<u>Can't be done</u>," he said. "It's only possible after a heavy snowfall. On our sands, after it snows, I sweep clear a patch of ground, prop up a big threshing basket with a short stick, and scatter husks of grain beneath.

5. 表否定意义的词汇

一些词汇表否定意义，但并非否定形式，如下面几例中的 unintentional, clueless, too…to 结构等。

原文：作为名目，即使与古人所撰《书法正传》的"正传"字面上很相混，也<u>顾不得了</u>。

蓝译本：Any similarity between the present work and the unforgettable Real Story of Calligraphy, by Mr Feng Wu of the Qing dynasty, is entirely <u>unintentional</u>.

杨译本：…and if this is reminiscent of the True Story of Calligraphy of the ancients, it <u>cannot</u> be helped.

原文：哼，可是读了一年，连"恶毒妇"也不懂，大约仍然是念死书。

蓝译本：He's been there a year, and look at him: <u>clueless</u>. I bet they just stuff the classics down their throats the whole time.

杨译本：But—bah!—after one whole year of study he <u>can't</u> even understand o-du-fu! He must still be studying dead books.

原文："你<u>不能</u>用小一点的箭头的么？"

蓝译本："…it was <u>too big</u> for such a small bird."

杨译本："<u>Can't</u> you use smaller arrows？"

6. 表肯定意义的词汇

表肯定的表达结合特定的语境也是可选的策略，如下例。

原文："……假洋鬼子的老婆会和没有辫子的男人睡觉，吓，<u>不是好东西</u>！"

蓝译本："…Hmm: the Fake Foreign Devil's wife... any woman willing to sleep with a man without a queue <u>must be a slut</u>！"

杨译本："The Imitation Foreign Devil's wife is willing to sleep with a man without a pigtail, hah! She <u>can't</u> be a good woman! …"

原文:"放屁!——不过乌老鸦的炸酱面确也不好吃,难怪她忍不住……"

蓝译本:"Balderdash! But I can understand why she was fed up with crow in fried-bean sauce..."

杨译本:"Nonsense! The fact is, those noodles with crow sauce were uneatable. I can't blame her for not being able to stomach them..."

原文:"想来你也无法可想。我也还得赶紧寻点事情做……"

蓝译本:"But you've problems of your own. I've got to find myself a job – and quickly."

杨译本:"I suppose you can't help? I shall have to find something to do very soon."

7. 其他形式的熟语

蓝译本还擅长使用一些熟语,也能起到相当的效果。

原文:阿Q看见自己的勋业得了赏识,便愈加兴高采烈起来:"和尚动得,我动不得?"他扭住伊的面颊。

蓝译本:"Sauce for the goose, sauce for the gander!" he quipped, now pinching her cheek, delighted his remarkable exploits were getting the recognition they deserved.

杨译本:Seeing that his feat was admired, Ah Q began to feel elated. "If the monk paws you, why can't I?" said he, pinching her cheek.

从上述译例可以看出,蓝译本的情态动词否定形式比杨译本更加多样,表达更加丰富。

本章小结

(1)与母语译者相比,非母语译者更倾向于使用情态动词。通过比较蓝译本与杨译本对鲁迅小说中情态动词"应该"的处理,我们可以看出,数量上,蓝译本更少使用情态动词;类别上,蓝译本的情态动词更加多样;翻译策略上,杨译本策略偏向直译,常使用should与原文的"应该"对应,而蓝译本则大量使用非情态动词的谓语结构,不拘泥于原文,更加灵活。

（2）非母语译者使用更多省略形式的情态动词，共 204 例，母语译者只有 16 例，二者悬殊巨大。这从侧面说明，母语译者的词汇文体更为正式。

（3）非母语译者更偏向使用由否定副词 not 构成的否定态。非母语译者共使用 685 个，远高于母语译者的 386 个。我们通过对比鲁迅小说两译本情态动词 can 的否定形式发现，杨译本有 61 例，而蓝译本共计只有 3 例，悬殊巨大。经过进一步对比发现，在杨译本使用 can't 的地方，蓝译本采用了更加灵活的应对方案，其中包括其他情态动词的否定形式、非情态动词的否定形式、非动词的否定形式、表否定意义的词汇、表肯定意义的词汇、其他形式的熟语等。

第九章　介词与连词使用对比

本章考察两类译者译本中介词与连词的使用特征。介词用来表示名词、代词等与句中其他词的关系，不能单独作句子成分。介词后面一般有名词、代词或相当于名词的其他词类、短语或从句作它的宾语，表示与其他成分的关系。

英语造句主要讲究形合（Hypotaxis）。所谓形合，指的是句中的词语或分句之间用语言形式手段连接。介词是重要的形合手段。据统计，英语各类介词（简单介词、合成介词与成语介词）共约 286 个。介词是英语里最活跃的词类之一，是连接词语或从句的重要手段（连淑能，2000）。沈家煊（1984）也指出，英语介词用法多样，使用频繁。英语里用介词的地方汉语常常不用介词，或者用动词。

连词是一种虚词，不能独立担任句子成分而只起连接词与词、短语与短语以及句与句的作用。连词主要可分为 4 类：并列连词、转折连词、选择连词和因果连词。汉语是意合语言，行文以松散的小句为主。因此相对介词而言，汉语连词使用更为频繁。

鉴于两种语言的区别，我们在考察汉语小说英译母语译者与非母语译者二者词汇文体差异时，可合理推测：母语译者可能更偏向使用介词，其使用的语境可能更加丰富；非母语译者或许会受汉语意合特征的影响，更倾向于使用连接形式相对较为松散的连词。

"关键值"是评估文本中词汇关键度的数值。我们对两类译者译本中的介词与连词进行统计，对比关键值，数据如下表所示。

表9.1 母语－非母语译者译本中介词与连词统计对比

序号	母语译者			非母语译者		
	出现次数	关键值	词语	出现次数	关键值	词语
1	8488	107.691	of	181	66.71	although
2	200	51.501	around	10056	40.373	and
3	323	21.179	through	113	37.598	till
4	696	20.91	about	113	20.743	nor
5	893	20.366	into	54	19.888	yet
6	39	12.427	beyond	328	19.64	because
7	32	9.982	despite	26	13.668	besides
8	7	9.008	alongside	840	9.937	after
9	53	8.436	within	2125	8.641	but
10	1541	6.845	from	153	7.383	under

我们提取出译本中的介词与连词，统计各自译者群体关键值排前十的单词。结果发现，母语译者关键值排前十的单词均为介词，其中 of 关键值最高，其次为 around, through, about, into 等。相比之下，非母语译者关键值排前十的单词中，仅有 after 和 under 为比较典型的介词，besides 兼作介词与连词，其他皆为连词。其中，although 关键值最高。

下面，我们以鲁迅小说为例，对比、分析两类译本关键介词与连词的使用频率与语境。

一、介词

（一）around 与 through 统计对比

我们重点考察 around 与 through 两个介词。因为二者关键性较高，使用频率相对较高，其数据统计可行性较能得到保障。

表9.2 鲁迅小说蓝译本与杨译本 around 和 through 统计对比

	around	through
蓝译本	102	107
杨译本	30	57

从上表数据可以看出，蓝译本中使用 around 共计 102 次，涉及共 7 种意义；相比而言，杨译本使用 30 次，涉及 5 种意义。从介词 around 的使用情况来看，蓝译本偏向使用更多介词，意义更加丰富。

（二）around 译例示范

1. 蓝译本中具体意义及用例示范

（1）大约（时间）

原文：那是赵太爷的儿子进了秀才的时候……

蓝译本：The whole business reared its head, as I recall, **around the time** that Mr Zhao's son had romped through the lowest, county-level stage of the civil service examination.

（2）在……身边

原文：虽然挨了打，大家也还怕有些真，总不如尊敬一些稳当。

蓝译本：Even though he had been soundly beaten for it, maybe everyone feared there might some grain of truth to the allegation, and the safest thing would be to **mind themselves around him** a bit more.

（3）到处

原文：……这话是未庄的乡下人从来不用，专是见过官府的阔人用的……

蓝译本：No common-or-garden term of abuse **around Weizhuang**, it was a usage favoured by the well-to-do, by those with official connections.

（4）围绕；环绕

原文：阿 Q 迟疑了一会，四面一看，并没有人。

蓝译本：Ah-Q hesitated, **glancing around him**: there was nobody about.

（5）绕过

原文：我提着两包闻喜名产的煮饼，走了许多潮湿的路，让道给许多拦路高卧的狗，这才总算到了连殳的门前。

蓝译本：I walked along a succession of damp streets and **around** a succession of dozing dogs, bearing two packages containing the steamed cakes for which Wenxi is renowned, until I finally reached Lianshu's gate.

（6）在……附近

原文：掌柜说，样子太傻，怕侍候不了长衫主顾，就在外面做点事罢。

蓝译本：But the manager said I looked too dull to wait on his prized long-gowned customers, and deployed me instead **around** the main bar.

（7）闲散地；无目的地

原文：……没有别的事，却闲着了，坐着只看柳妈洗器皿。

蓝译本：Xianglin's wife **sat** idly **around**, watching the fire, then watching Mrs Liu at work.

2. 杨译本中具体意义及用例示范

（1）向四周

原文：阿Q迟疑了一会，四面一看，并没有人。

杨译本：Ah Q hesitated for a time, looking **around** him. Since there was no one in sight…

（2）向各处

原文：他们可以问去，全衙门里什么人也没有领到，都得初八！

杨译本：They can ask **around**. Nobody in the yamen will be paid until the eighth.

（3）到四周

原文：我写包票！船又大；迅哥儿向来不乱跑；我们又都是识水性的！

杨译本：I give my word it'll be all right! It's a big boat, Brother Hsun never **jumps around**, and we can all swim!

（4）掉头

原文：三四人径奔船尾，拔了篙，点退几丈，回转船头……

杨译本：Three or four boys ran to the stern, seized the poles to punt back several yards, and headed the boat **around**.

（5）围绕着

原文：他听得呜咽声高了起来，也就站了起来，钻过门幕，想着，"马克思在儿女的啼哭声中还会做《资本论》，所以他是伟人……

杨译本：Hearing the sobs increase in volume, he stood up and brushed past the curtain, thinking, "Karl Marx wrote his Das Kapital while his children were crying **around** him. He must really have been a great man…"

二、连词

我们考察鲁迅小说两个英译本对"因为"（表因果）和"虽然"（表转折）两个连词的英译。

（一）连词"因为"英译分析

原文中"因为"共出现168次，其英译策略有6种情况，分别译为：连词、介词、谓语结构、ing分词结构、定语结构和省略。统计数据如下。

表9.3 蓝译本与杨译本"因为"英译情况统计

译文	蓝译本		杨译本	
	数量	类别	数量	类别
连词	55	4	113	5
介词	14	8	21	10
ing分词结构	1	1	0	0
谓语结构	9	8	2	2
定语结构	1	1	0	0
其他短语/句子结构	0	0	3	2
省略	77	/	18	/
合计	157	/	157	/

1. 译为连词

将"因为"译为英语中的连词,共有 5 种:because, for, as, since, now that。蓝译本共使用 55 个连词,杨译本使用了 113 个连词,是蓝译本的 2 倍以上。译例如下:

(1) because

原文:<u>因为</u>未庄的人们之于阿 Q,只要他帮忙,只拿他玩笑,从来没有留心他的"行状"的。

蓝译本:**Because** the good people of Weizhuang called upon him only to help out with odd jobs, or to serve as the butt of jokes, no one ever paid much attention to such niceties.

蓝译本共使用 50 个连词 because 来翻译"因为",杨译本则使用了 88 个。

(2) for

原文:其次是赵府,非特秀才<u>因为</u>上城去报官,被不好的革命党剪了辫子……

蓝译本:Next in line were the Zhaos, **for** not only did the village genius have his queue cut off by rogue revolutionaries when he went into town to report the crime…

蓝译本共使用 2 个连词 for,而杨译本则使用了 17 个,远高于蓝译本。

(3) since

原文:我们年纪都相仿,但论起行辈来,却至少是叔子,有几个还是太公,<u>因为</u>他们合村都同姓,是本家。

蓝译本:Though we were all of an age, most of them were born one or even two generations above me, and **since** everyone in the village shared the same surname, we were all of the same, loose clan.

蓝译本共使用 1 个连词 since,而杨译本则使用了 5 个。

(4) as

原文:起先我们选择得很苛酷——也非苛酷,<u>因为</u>看去大抵不像是我们的安身之所……

蓝译本：At the beginning of our search, we were very particular – or perhaps not particular enough, **as** we wouldn't have felt welcome in most of the rooms we looked at.

蓝译本共使用 2 个连词 as，杨译本也使用了 2 个。

（5）now that

原文：有时连饭也不够，虽然我因为终日坐在家里用脑，饭量已经比先前要减少得多。

杨译本：My appetite was much smaller than before, **now that** I was sitting at home all day using my brain, but even so there wasn't always even enough rice.

杨译本共使用 1 个连词 now that，而蓝译本则未使用。

2. 译为介词（短语）

将"因为"译为英语中的介词（短语），共有 12 种情况：for, in, from, after, because of, on account of, for fear of, out of, thanks to, owing to, in order to, in the interests of。蓝译本共使用 14 次介词，杨译本使用了 21 次介词。译例如下：

（1）for

原文：但不知道因为什么，又并不叫他洋先生。

蓝译本：**For** some reason, at the last moment he decided against Mr Foreigner.

蓝译本使用了 2 个介词 for，杨译本使用了 1 个。

（2）from

原文：她当时的勇敢和无畏是因为爱。

蓝译本：Back then, she had drawn her courage **from** love.

蓝译本使用介词 from 共 1 次，杨译本未使用。

（3）after

原文：离平桥村还有一里模样，船行却慢了，摇船的都说很疲乏，因为太用力，而且许久没有东西吃。

杨译本：We were still about a third of a mile from Pingchiao when our boat slowed down, and the oarsmen said they were tired **after** rowing so hard. We'd had nothing to eat for hours.

杨译本使用 after 共 1 次，蓝译本未使用。

（4）in

原文：这回因为正气忿，因为要报仇，便不由的轻轻的说出来了。

蓝译本：This time, however, **in** his furious desire for revenge against a harsh, cruel world, they crept softly out into the open.

蓝译本和杨译本各用 1 次 in 来表"因为"。

（5）because of

原文：因为王胡以络腮胡子的缺点，向来只被他奚落，从没有奚落他，更不必说动手了。

蓝译本：**Because of** the man's appalling whiskers, he had never had anything but pitying contempt for this Wang, who was too contemptible even to despise him back – much less raise a hand against him.

蓝译本使用 6 次，杨译本使用 7 次。

（6）for fear （of/that）

原文：有一位本家，还预备去告官，但后来因为恐怕革命党的造反或者要成功，这才中止了。

杨译本：One of my own family planned to indict me, but he later refrained from doing this **for** fear the rebels of the revolutionary party might succeed.

杨译本使用 3 次，蓝译本使用 0 次。

（7）out of

原文：羿忽然心惊肉跳起来，觉得嫦娥是因为气忿寻了短见了……

蓝译本：Yi's heart began to pound: could Chang'e have committed suicide **out of** pique?

蓝译本和杨译本各用 1 次 out of 来表"因为"。

（8）on account of

原文：赵秀才本也想靠着寄存箱子的渊源，亲身去拜访举人老爷的，但因为有剪辫的危险，所以也中止了。

蓝译本：On the pretext of the trunks he was giving house-room to, the Zhao family's young gentleman of letters had thought of calling on Mr. Provincial Examination, but desisted on account of the mortal risk to his queue.

蓝译本使用 1 次，杨译本使用 3 次。

（9）in the interest of

原文：我因为生计关系，不得不一早在路上走。

蓝译本：Early each morning, **in the interests of** making a living, I would take myself on to the almost deserted streets of Beijing…

蓝译本使用 1 次，杨译本未使用。

（10）owing to

原文：他自己虽然不知道是因为懒，还是因为无用，总之觉得是一个不肯运动，十分安分守己的人。

杨译本：Although not knowing himself whether **owing to** indolence, or because it was useless, at all events he refused to take part in movements and regarded himself as thoroughly law-abiding.

杨译本使用 1 次，蓝译本未使用。

（11）thanks to

原文：那时人说：因为伊，这豆腐店的买卖非常好。

蓝译本：Everyone used to say back then that it was **thanks to** her the bean-curd shop turned over such a tidy profit.

蓝译本使用 1 次，杨译本使用 2 次。

（12）in order to

原文：我的话还没有完哩。你对于我们，偶而来访问你的我们，也以为因为闲着无事，所以来你这里，将你当作消遣的资料的罢？

杨译本：I haven't finished yet. I suppose you consider people like me, who come here occasionally, do so **in order to** kill time or amuse themselves at your expense?

杨译本使用1次，蓝译本未使用。

3. 译为 -ing 分词结构

原文：我在倒数上去的二十年中，只看过两回中国戏，前十年是绝不看，因为没有看戏的意思和机会。

蓝译本：Counting back through the last twenty years, I've seen only two Chinese operas – and neither of them in the first ten, **finding** myself without the desire or the opportunity to do so.

蓝译本使用1次，杨译本未使用。

4. 译为谓语结构

（1）go back to

原文：穿凿起来说，或者因为阿Q说是赵太爷的本家。

蓝译本：Perhaps—to hazard an unreliable guess at the matter—it all **went back to** AH-Q's claim of blood relation to Mr Zhao.

蓝译本使用1次，杨译本0次。

（2）tell

原文：我想，这回定是酒客了，因为听得那脚步声比堂倌的要缓得多。

蓝译本：At last, however, a series of footsteps much slower than the waiter's **told** me another patron was on his way up.

蓝译本使用1次，杨译本0次。

（3）contribute to

原文：但因为他没有家小，家中究竟非常寂寞，这大概也就是大家所谓异样之一端罢。

蓝译本：Probably his own failure to have a family and the solitude in which he lived **contributed to** his reputation for eccentricity.

蓝译本使用 1 次，杨译本 0 次。

（4）motivate

原文：恐怕大半也还是因为好奇心，我归途中经过他家的门口，便又顺便去吊慰。

蓝译本：**Motivated** substantially **by** curiosity, I'm afraid, I made sure my way home took me past his front door, taking the opportunity to offer my condolences.

蓝译本使用 1 次，杨译本 0 次。

（5）make

原文：他因为事情忙，是早就废止了朝食的……

蓝译本：A long time ago, the demands of hunting had **made** breakfast an impossible luxury…

蓝译本使用 2 次，杨译本 1 次。

（6）hurry on

原文：仿佛记得心里也一动，或者也许放慢了脚步的罢，但似乎因为舍不得皮夹里仅存的六角钱，所以竟也毅然决然的走远了。

蓝译本：But even as he slowed down, a reluctance to part with the last sixty cents in his wallet **hurried him** resolutely **on**.

蓝译本使用 1 次，杨译本 0 次。

（7）prevent sb from doing sth.

原文：其实，我一个人，是容易生活的，虽然因为骄傲，向来不与世交来往，迁居以后，也疏远了所有旧识的人。

蓝译本：If I'd been on my own, I'd have easily made a living. My pride had **prevented** me **from** having much to do with old family friends, and since moving out of the hostel I'd neglected all my former acquaintances.

蓝译本使用 1 次，杨译本 0 次。

（8）protect against

原文：他五六年前，曾在戏台下的人丛中拧过一个女人的大腿，但因为隔一层裤，所以此后并不飘飘然……

蓝译本：Some five or six years past, wedged within a packed opera audience, he had taken the opportunity to pinch a woman's thigh, but her intervening trousers had **protected against** this debilitating light-headedness.

蓝译本使用1次，杨译本0次。

（9）attribute… to

原文：这在阿Q，或者以为因为他是赵太爷的父亲，而其实也不然。

杨译本：He probably **attributed** this **to** the fact that he was Mr. Chao's father, but actually such was not the case.

杨译本使用1次，蓝译本0次。

5. 译为定语结构

原文：因为文体卑下，是"引车卖浆者流"所用的话，所以不敢僭称……

蓝译本：…and yet the **debased vulgarity** of its content and characters causes me to shy, appalled, from such presumption.

蓝译本1次，杨译本0次。

6. 译为其他短语/句子结构

（1）too… to 句型

原文：其实，我一个人，是容易生活的，虽然因为骄傲，向来不与世交来往。

杨译本：Actually, when I was on my own I had got along very well, although I was **too** proud **to** mix much with family acquaintances. But since my move I had become estranged from all my old friends.

杨译本1次，蓝译本0次。

（2）the reason… is… 句型

原文：我终日如坐在冰窖子里，如站在刑场旁边，其实并非别的，只**因**为缺少了一条辫子！

杨译本：I felt as if sitting all day in an ice-house, or standing by an execution ground. And the sole **reason for this was** my lack of a queue!

杨译本2次，蓝译本0次。

（3）it is that...句型

原文：她大约**因**为在别人的祝福时候，感到自身的寂寞了，然而会不会含有别的什么意思的呢？

杨译本：Probably **it is just that** when other people are celebrating she feels lonely by herself, but could there be another reason?

杨译本1次，蓝译本0次。

（4）省略

原文：阿Q奔入舂米场，一个人站着，还觉得指头痛，还记得"忘八蛋"，**因**为这话是未庄的乡下人从来不用，专是见过官府的阔人用的。

蓝译本：His fingers still stinging, Ah-Q took solitary refuge in the rice-husking room, feeling deeply unsettled by this "bastard". No common-or-garden term of abuse around Weizhuang, it was a usage favoured by the well-to-do, by those with official connections.

蓝译本77次，杨译本18次。

从上面的数据统计与译例分析可以看出，原文中的连词"因为"在蓝译本中的英译更为丰富、多样。

（二）连词"虽然"英译分析

鲁迅小说原文中共计有"虽（然）"120处。蓝译本共使用14种翻译方法，其中包括：although（22）；even though（15）；even if（2）；though（7）；still（2）；for（1）；despite（4）；however（2）；might（1）；it was...that（1）；for all（1）；but（5）；yet（2）；省略（55）。杨译本共使用13种翻译方法，其中包

括: although（80）; even though（3）; even if（1）; though（8）; in spite of（1）; despite（1）; while（1）; might（2）; but（1）; yet（2）; even so（1）; even（2）; 省略（17）。数据如下表所示。

表9.4 蓝译本与杨译本"虽然"英译情况统计

类别	用词	蓝译本	杨译本
连词	although	22	80
	though	7	8
	even though	15	3
	even if	2	1
	even so	0	1
	however	2	0
	but	5	1
	yet	2	2
	while	0	1
	still	2	0
小计		57	97
其他	for	1	0
	in spite of	0	1
	despite	4	1
	might	1	2
	for all	1	0
	even	0	2
	it was…that	1	0
省略		55	17
合计		120	120

具体译例示范如下:

1. 译为 although

原文: 他<u>虽然</u>多住未庄,然而也常常宿在别处,不能说是未庄人,即使说是"未庄人也",也仍然有乖史法的。

蓝译本：**Although** he spent most of his life in the village of Weizhuang, he was often to be found in other places, too, so to term him with a native of Weizhuang would hardly be historically rigorous.

2. 译为 though

原文：他<u>虽然</u>自己并不看见装了怎样的脸，但此时却觉得很局促，嘴唇微微一动，又摇一摇头。

蓝译本：**Though** he couldn't conjure up the exact expression he had worn at the time, the memory was discomforting. He shook his head, his lips trembling slightly.

3. 译为 even though

原文：<u>虽然</u>挨了打，大家也还怕有些真，总不如尊敬一些稳当。

蓝译本：**Even though** he had been soundly beaten for it, maybe everyone feared there might some grain of truth to the allegation, and the safest thing would be to mind themselves around him a bit more.

4. 译为 even if

原文：有了四千年吃人履历的我，当初<u>虽然</u>不知道，现在明白，难见真的人！

蓝译本：With the weight of four thousand years of cannibalism bearing down upon me, **even if** once I was innocent how can I now face real humans?

5. 译为 even so

原文：这不过是他的一种新不平；<u>虽说</u>不平，又只是他的一种安分的空论。

杨译本：This was simply a new sense of injustice he had. **Even so**, it was just empty.

6. 译为 but

原文：<u>虽然</u>肚饿，心里却很喜欢，他们不喝鸡汤实在已经有一年多了。

蓝译本：He was famished **but** happy: neither of them had tasted chicken soup for over a year.

7. 译为 however

原文：但单四嫂子<u>虽然</u>粗笨，却知道还魂是不能有的事，他的宝儿也的确不能再见了。

蓝译本：But **however** simple and uneducated Mrs Shan was, she knew that the dead cannot come back to life; that she would never see her Bao'er again.

8. 译为 despite

原文：世界上并非没有为了奋斗者而开的活路；我也还未忘却翅子的扇动，<u>虽然</u>比先前已经颓唐得多……

蓝译本：A way forward always exists for those who are willing to fight for it. **Despite** all the setbacks, I hadn't yet forgotten how to flap my wings...

9. 译为 might

原文：他<u>虽然</u>是粗笨女人，心里却有决断…

杨译本：She **might** be a simple woman, but she had a will of her own.

10. 译为 even for

原文：倘使只知道捶着一个人的衣角，那便是<u>虽</u>战士也难于战斗，只得一同灭亡。

杨译本：All she could do was cling to someone else's clothing, making it difficult **even for** a fighter to struggle, and bringing ruin on both.

11. 译为 yet

原文：<u>虽然</u>幸而没有送掉性命，结果也还是躺在地上，只争着一个迟早之间。

蓝译本：… and **yet** not quite. But after it all, we had been left sprawled weakly over the ground, the end in clear sight.

12. 译为 for

原文：那女人<u>虽</u>是山里人模样，然而应酬很从容，说话也能干。

蓝译本：She conducted herself with unusual self-possession, **for** a peasant from the mountains.

13. 译为 for all

原文：九斤老太虽然高寿，耳朵却还不很聋，但也没有听到孩子的话，仍旧自己说……

蓝译本：Mrs Nine-Pounds's hearing was little impaired **for all** her seventy-eight years—but happily the girl's verdict escaped her ears.

14. 译为 while

原文：只是暗暗地告诫四姑说，这种人虽然似乎很可怜，但是败坏风俗的……

杨译本：…only secretly warned my aunt that **while** such people may seem very pitiful they exert a bad moral influence.

15. 译为 still

原文：这也不足为奇，中国的兴学虽说已经二十年了，寒石山却连小学也没有。

蓝译本：And no wonder. Twenty years after China had launched a national programme of educational reform, Hanshi Mountain **still** found itself without so much as a primary school.

16. 译为 in spite of

原文：不久也就仿佛是自己打了别个一般——虽然还有些热刺刺——心满意足的得胜的躺下了。

杨译本：…and soon it was just as if he had beaten someone else-**in spite of** the fact that his face was still tingling. He lay down satisfied that he had gained the victory.

17. 译为 it was…that

原文：然而阿Q虽然常优胜，却直待蒙赵太爷打他嘴巴之后，这才出了名。

蓝译本：In Ah-Q's long and illustrious record of victories, **it was** the slap he had received from Mr Zhao **that** made his reputation.

18. 省略

原文：否则，也如孔庙里的太牢一般，虽然与猪羊一样，同是畜生，但既经圣人下箸，先儒们便不敢妄动了。

蓝译本：Or maybe Ah-Q became as untouchable as the sacrificial beef in

Confucius's ancestral temple – because the sage had once touched it with his scared chopsticks, it acquired an aura of sanctity for his disciples.

从以上数据统计以及译例示范，可以看出，蓝译本使用 57 例连词，而杨译本使用 97 例，大大高于蓝译本；两译本使用最多的转折词均为 although，但蓝译本该词使用 22 例，而杨译本使用了 80 例，这表明，杨译本的翻译策略相对较为集中和单一；蓝译本在处理原文转折关系时，使用了 55 例省略策略，杨译本使用了 17 例，这一数据也从侧面印证了蓝译本倾向于摆脱原文的显性逻辑关系，翻译方法更为灵活。

本章小结

本章考察了母语译者与非母语译者在介词与连词使用方面的差异，主要研究对象为鲁迅小说的蓝译本和杨译本。通过系统的数据对比与译例比照，得出以下结论。

① 母语译者更加注重使用介词。以介词 around 为例，经统计，蓝译本共使用该介词 102 次，涉及 7 种意义；杨译本使用该介词共 30 次，涉及 5 种意义。

② 母语译者更少使用连词。本章重点考察了母语—非母语译者对"因为"（表因果）和"虽然"（表转折）两个连词的英译。原文中"因为"共有 168 次，蓝译本共使用 55 个连词，杨译本使用了 113 个连词，是蓝译本的 2 倍以上。针对原文中 120 处虽（然）；蓝译本使用连词 57 个，杨译本使用 97 个。

③ 母语译者翻译方法更加灵活。以连词"因为"的译法为例。两译本中，该词英译策略有 6 种情况，分别是：连词、介词、谓语结构、ing 分词结构、定语结构、省略。蓝译本使用了全部 6 种译法，杨译本只采用了 4 种方法，后者翻译手段相对集中和单一。

第十章　词汇搭配

词汇搭配对英语产出的流利性和地道性至关重要(Wu; Witten; Franken, 2010)。Cowie(1994)指出,如何区分本族语者与非本族语者的语言,能否恰当使用搭配已成为重要的区别标志。有学者认为,词语搭配能力的习得在英语学习的中高级阶段尤其重要。国内外若干现有研究表明,英语学习者与本族语者之间在词语搭配上存在系统性差异(Begagić, 2014; Crossley, Salsbury, Mcnamara, 2015; Martelli, 2006; Yan, 2010; 王海华、陈国华, 2007; 何影、梁茂成, 2010; 武光军, 2010)。搭配能力如此重要,却是二语教学中常被忽视的部分(Hashemi, 2014)。

毋庸置疑,词汇搭配也是衡量翻译能力的重要标准。翻译教学研究者常有一个错误的假定,即学习者已经具备了充足的语言能力,包括在词汇搭配方面没有障碍(Chukwu, 1997)。更有学者直言,搭配是译者的一个薄弱点(Bahumaid, 2006)。

多数研究从规约性视角,审视初、中级英语学习者或翻译学习者的词汇搭配能力,对于非本族语高级使用者的词汇搭配风格关注不多。

本章拟从副动搭配、量词词组以及 N of N 搭配入手,深入探讨母语和非母语译者之间的词汇搭配风格差异。本章研究的对象为鲁迅小说各译本。

一、副动搭配

副词指用以修饰动词、形容词、其他副词以及全句的词,表示时间、地点、程度、方式等概念。(薄冰,2000:397)各种语法书对副词界定不一。(Alexander, 1988; 薄冰,2000, 张道真,2002)此外,还有评价副词(evaluative adverb),

类似于观点副词和句子副词。(参见剑桥在线词典: https://dictionary.cambridge.org/)

本研究将副词分为两大类:一是次修饰型副词,指程度副词等,如 extremely;二是进一步描述型副词,指定性类形容词构成的副词,如 strangely。次修饰语型副词主要起到辅助性功能,并不增加实质性信息;而进一步描述型副词的信息量更大,修辞内涵更丰富。本研究将表方式、性质、态度等信息的副词与动词的搭配归类为进一步描述型搭配,而表达程度、频率等意义的副词与动词的搭配归类为次修饰型搭配。进一步描述性动副搭配又可细分为普通搭配与超常规搭配。所谓超常规搭配,指超越正常逻辑和情景的词语搭配,旨在表达某种特殊意味。超常规搭配是文学性语言较为青睐的搭配,在小说语言及其译文赏析中不可忽视。

(一)总体对比

我们对比鲁迅小说两类译者副动搭配使用情况,统计如下:

表 10.1 母语—非母语译者译本副动搭配使用对比统计

搭配	母语译者	非母语译者	蓝译本	杨译本
动词 + 副词	3538	3514	999	1156
副词 + 动词	4171	3948	1279	1238
合计	7709	7462	2278	2394

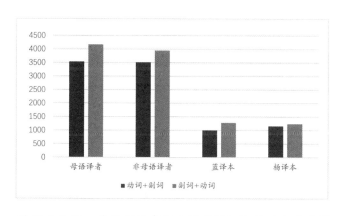

图 10.1 母语—非母语译者译本副动搭配使用对比示意图

从统计对比来看，母语译者译本副动搭配略多于非母语译者译本，多 247 例；但鲁迅小说的蓝译本与杨译本相比，杨译本使用更多副动搭配。

（二）进一步描述型副动搭配

我们统计了进一步描述型副词与动词的搭配情况，并进行重点研究。该类型副词主要组成为 -ly 型副词。

表 10.2 鲁迅小说不同译本副动搭配使用对比统计

搭配	母语译者	非母语译者	蓝译本	杨译本
动词 +ly 副词	874	687	326	253
ly 副词 + 动词	1476	1265	491	411
合计	2350	1952	817	664

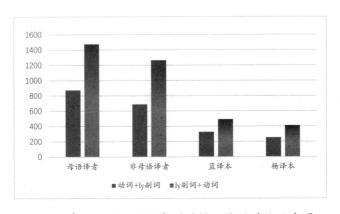

图 10.2 鲁迅小说不同译本副动搭配使用对比示意图

-ly 型副词与动词的搭配在母语译者译本中出现频率更高。

我们聚焦鲁迅小说蓝译本与杨译本中带有超常色彩的进一步描述型副动搭配。蓝译本中该类搭配共 23 例，杨译本中 7 例，远少于前者。具体译例如下。

1. 蓝译本进一步描述型副动搭配

（1）cracked emphatically

原文：果然，拍的一声，似乎确凿打在自己头上了。

蓝译本：Predictably enough, a hard object **cracked emphatically** against his head.

（2）drooping visibly

原文：穿的是新夹袄，看去腰间还挂着一个大搭连，沉钿钿的将裤带坠成了很弯很弯的弧线。

蓝译本：He had on a new cotton jacket, his belt **drooping visibly** from the weight of the purse at his waist.

（3）flashing fiendishly

原文：可是永远记得那狼眼睛，又凶又怯，闪闪的像两颗鬼火，似乎远远的来穿透了他的皮肉。

蓝译本：He had never forgotten the wolf's eyes, fierce and cowardly, **flashing fiendishly**, burning into his flesh.

（4）managed miserably

原文："回去罢。"他迟疑了片时，这才悲惨的说。

蓝译本："Off you go," he **managed miserably**, after a brief hesitation.

（5）shone uncomfortably

原文：刚近房门，却看见满眼都明亮，连一群鸡也正在笑他……

蓝译本：But as he approached, the light **shone uncomfortably** in his eyes again and a flock of chickens cackled with laughter.

（6）bore alarmingly down

原文："那倒不然，而孰知不然！"薇园摊开手掌，向四铭连摇带推的奔过去，力争说。

蓝译本："Out of the question!" Weiyuan now **bore alarmingly down** on Siming, presenting his flattened palm in a gesture of refusal.

（7）stood uselessly

原文：迟疑了一会，就有几个人上前去劝止他，愈去愈多，终于挤成一大堆。

蓝译本：Eventually the bewildered villagers edged forward, to try to get him to stop, until a great crowd of them **stood uselessly** about him.

（8）swirling uselessly

原文：但又总觉得被什么挡着似的，单在脑里面回旋，吐不出口外去。

蓝译本：But something seemed to be stopping them come out, leaving them **swirling uselessly** about inside my head.

（9）Smiling broadly

原文：因大笑，出示日记二册，谓可见当日病状，不妨献诸旧友。

蓝译本：**Smiling broadly**, he showed me two volumes of a diary his brother had written at the time, explaining that they would give me an idea of the sickness that had taken hold of him and that he saw no harm in showing them to an old friend.

（10）clinging clammily

原文：没奈何坐在路旁一家公馆的门槛上，休息了一会，衣服渐渐的冰着肌肤……

蓝译本：Eventually, she sat down to rest at the threshold of one of the village's better establishments, her clothes **clinging clammily** to her...

（11）sitting blankly

原文：单四嫂子张着眼，呆呆坐着。

蓝译本：Mrs Shan went on **sitting blankly**.

（12）luxuriating nostalgically

原文：我们只在灯下对坐的怀旧谭中，回味那时冲突以后的和解的重生一般的乐趣。

蓝译本：Now all we did was sit by the lamp opposite each other, going back over old times, **luxuriating nostalgically** in the pleasurable memory of reconciliation.

（13）chewed obliviously

原文：即使在坐中给看一点怒色，她总是不改变，仍然毫无感触似的大嚼起来。

蓝译本：I tried glaring at her at mealtimes, but she just **chewed obliviously** on.

（14）sprawled weakly

原文：虽然幸而没有送掉性命，结果也还是躺在地上，只争着一个迟早之间。

蓝译本：But after it all, we had been left **sprawled weakly** over the ground, the end in clear sight.

（15）striding obliviously

原文：这一夜，就是我对于中国戏告了别的一夜，此后再没有想到他，即使偶而经过戏园，我们也漠不相关，精神上早已一在天之南一在地之北了。

蓝译本：That night, I bade farewell for ever to Chinese opera. And for years, I never gave it so much as a thought, **striding obliviously** past the capital's theatres as if they existed in a parallel dimension.

（16）needlessly involved

原文：又没有别人看见，便很怪他多事，要自己惹出是非，也误了我的路。

蓝译本：And that no one else had seen it happen, I felt only irritation at my runner for getting **needlessly involved**. He would make trouble for himself, and hold me up – quit unnecessarily.

（17）clinging lustrously

原文：我这时又忽地想到这里积雪的滋润，著物不去……

蓝译本：I was reminded again of the nourishing moisture of southern snow – **clinging lustrously** to anything it touches…

（18）looking unsuccessfully about

原文：四叔踱出门外，也不见，一直到河边，才见平平正正的放在岸上，旁边还有一株菜。

蓝译本：After **looking unsuccessfully about** outside, Uncle walked all the way down to the river, where at last he found it, sitting upright on the bank, next to a bunch of vegetables.

（19）trying unsuccessfully

原文：她转了几个圆圈，终于没有事情做，只得疑惑的走开。

蓝译本：Xianglin's wife circled about, **trying unsuccessfully** to find something she could do, then walked dazedly off.

（20）hanging stupidly

原文：她张着口怔怔的站着，直着眼睛看他们，接着也就走了，似乎自己也觉得没趣。

蓝译本：She would stand there, mouth **hanging stupidly** open, watching as they distanced themselves, before moving on herself – as if she, too, were bored with her own tragedy.

（21）chewed deliciously

原文：她未必知道她的悲哀经大家咀嚼赏鉴了许多天，早已成为渣滓，只值得烦厌和唾弃。

蓝译本：Perhaps it hadn't yet dawned on her that her sorrow, having been **chewed deliciously** for so long, had now been reduced to dregs, to be spat out in disgust.

（22）gleamed phosphorescently

原文：后面远处有银白的条纹，是月亮已从那边出现；前面却仅有两点磷火一般的那黑色人的眼光。

蓝译本：Far behind him lay the silver rays of the rising moon. In front, the stranger's eyes **gleamed phosphorescently** in the darkness.

（23）rushing uselessly about

原文：上自王后，下至弄臣，也都恍然大悟，仓皇散开，急得手足无措，各自转了四五个圈子。

蓝译本：Everyone – from the queen down to the court jester – scattered, **rushing uselessly about** in panicked circles.

2. 杨译本进一步描述型副动搭配

（1）advancing menacingly

原文：赵太爷愈看愈生气了，抢进几步说："你敢胡说！"

杨译本：The more he looked at him the angrier Mr. Chao became, and **advancing**

menacingly a few steps he said, "How dare you talk such nonsense!"

（2）shambled disconsolately

原文：他不自觉的旋转了觉得涣散了身躯，悯悯的走向归家的路。

杨译本：Not knowing what he did, he turned with a strange sensation of disintegration, and **shambled disconsolately** home.

（3）grunting noncommittally

原文：我很劝慰了一番；他却除了唯唯诺诺之外，只回答了一句话，是："多谢你的好意。"

杨译本：I urged him not to take it so to heart, but apart from **grunting noncommittally** all he said was: "Thanks for your concern."

（4）decided tentatively

原文：他想来想去，想不出好地方，便要假定为 A 了。

杨译本：He racked his brains but, unable to think of a good place, **decided tentatively** to fix on A.

（5）stared vacantly around

原文：那老女人徘徊观望了一回，忽然手脚有些发抖，跄跄踉踉退下几步，瞪着眼只是发怔。

杨译本：The older woman took a few aimless steps and **stared vacantly around**, then suddenly she began to tremble and stagger backwards, as though giddy.

（6）clung lingeringly

原文：无论那边的干雪怎样纷飞，这里的柔雪又怎样的依恋，于我都没有什么关系了。

杨译本：The dry snow up there, which flew like powder, and the soft snow here, which **clung lingeringly**, seemed equally alien to me.

（7）perched kittenishly

原文：幸而她撒娇坐在他的御膝上，特别扭了七十多回，这才使龙眉之间的皱纹渐渐地舒展。

杨译本：Fortunately, **perched kittenishly** on the royal knee, she wriggled over seventy times till at last the wrinkles on the kingly brow were smoothed out.

二、量名搭配

（一）总体对比

我们对比两类译本中的 a / an + 量词 + of 型量词表达，发现母语译者使用更多该类搭配，统计如下：

表 10.3 母语—非母语译者译本量词结构使用对比统计

搭配	母语译者	非母语译者	蓝译本	杨译本
a/an + 名词 + of	544	440	159	108

我们将鲁迅小说蓝、杨译本中的该类表达类型提取出来，并做统计对比。蓝译本使用 159 例该类表达，共计 65 种；杨译本共使用 108 例，共计 53 种。可以看出，蓝译本中的量词表达更为丰富一些。具体如下：

蓝译本（65/159）	杨译本（53/108）
an armful of / a bag of / a basket of / a bit of / a bottle of / a bowl of / a bunch of / a bustle of / a chain of / a clatter of / a cluster of / a cocoon of / a column of / a confusion of / a copse of / a couple of / a crowd of / a cup of / an edge of / a flask of / a flock of / a gang of / a glimmer of / a gob of / a handful of / a hank of / a heap of / a hive of / a layer of / a load of / a lot of / a mass of / a mouthful of / a number of / a pack of / a packet of / a pair of / a patch of / a peal of / a piece of / a pile of / a plate of / a pot of / a ray of / a roar of / a rush of / a saucer of / a scattering of / a sea of / a series of / a shaft of / a sip of / a slip of / a squad of / a stretch of / a stroke of / a team of / a tower of / a trickle of / a twinge of / a variety of	a basket of / a bit of / a bottle of / a bowl of / a bundle of / a cent of / a chain of / a chip of / a clatter of / a clump of / a confusion of / a council of / a couple of / a crowd of / a cup of / a dipperful of / a dish of / an expanse of / a flash of / a freight of / a group of / a handful of / a heap of / a host of / a hum of / a kind of / a lot of / a mark of / a morsel of / a mound of / a number of / a package of / a packet of / a pair of / a patch of / a piece of/ a pile of/ a poolful of / a pot of / a press of / a procession of / a sea of / a selection of / a series of / a sheet of / a sip of / a slip of / a squad of / a streak of / a string of / a sum of / a swarm of / a volume of

(二)译例解析

英语中有大量比喻式量名搭配,这些表达为译文增添了文学色彩。我们比较两译本中的比喻式量名搭配,结构为"a / an + 量词 + of + 名词",蓝译本中该类搭配为 10 项,杨译本中仅有 2 项,二者有较大悬殊。

1. 蓝译本中比喻式量名搭配

(1) a twinge of desire

原文:他在路上走着要"求食",看见熟识的酒店,看见熟识的馒头,但他都走过了,不但没有暂停,而且并不想要。

蓝译本:He walked past familiar sights – the tavern, trays of steamed rolls– without pausing, without registering **a twinge of desire** for either.

(2) a stretch of time

原文:有一年的秋天,我在寒石山的一个亲戚家里闲住;他们就姓魏,是连殳的本家。

蓝译本:One autumn, I happened to find myself idling **a stretch of time** away with some relatives who lived near Hanshi Mountain, and who, sharing the surname Wei, happened also to claim a distant relation to Wei Lianshu.

(3) a cocoon of loneliness

原文:"那你可错误了。人们其实并不这样。你实在亲手造了独头茧,将自己裹在里面了。原文:你应该将世间看得光明些。"我叹惜着说。

蓝译本:"Well, you're wrong," I sighed. "People aren't like that. You've spun **a cocoon of loneliness** around yourself. Can't you try to see the bright side of things?"

(4) a glimmer of unhappiness

原文:这就使我也一样地不快活,傍晚回来,常见她包藏着不快活的颜色,尤其使我不乐的是她要装作勉强的笑容。

蓝译本:Sometimes, on returning home of an evening, I'd catch **a glimmer of unhappiness** on her face, her painfully forced smile grieving me particularly.

（5）a sea of pigtails

原文：呵！不得了了，人言啧啧了；我却只装作不知道，一任他们光着头皮，和许多辫子一齐上讲堂。

蓝译本：Everyone was talking about it, but I had to pretend I didn't know a thing, just let them sit through my classes – the only crew-cuts in **a sea of pigtails**.

（6）an edge of impatience

原文：我觉得母亲实在太修善，于是不由的就说出模棱的近乎不以为然的答话来。

蓝译本：Mother, I felt, was far too soft on them – which is why I allowed **an edge of impatience** into my reply.

（7）a shaft of sunlight

原文：做不做全由自己的便；那作品，像太阳的光一样，从无量的光源中涌出来，不像石火，用铁和石敲出来，这才是真艺术。

蓝译本：whatever he writes – or chooses not to write – is an expression of the self; **a shaft of sunlight** blazing out from an infinite light source, not the occasional spark struck from a flint.

（8）a roar of movement

原文：静了一会，似乎有点声音，便又动摇起来，轰的一声，都向后退；一直散到老栓立着的地方，几乎将他挤倒了。

蓝译本：A moment's silence, a slight noise, then they regained the power of motion. With **a roar of movement**, the mass of them pushed back towards Shuan, almost sweeping him over in the crush.

（9）a hive of activity

原文：鲁镇永远是过新年，腊月二十以后就火起来了。

蓝译本：Around ten days before New Year, Luzhen always turned into **a hive of activity**.

（10）a sea of blood

原文：彼用百头颅，千头颅兮用万头颅！我用一头颅兮而无万夫。爱一头颅兮血乎呜呼！

蓝译本：The king lets loose **a sea of blood**. I but a droplet or a stream. Yet I love this head: of blood I dream.

2. 杨译本中比喻式量名搭配

（1）a mound of cabbages

原文：就在他背后的书架的旁边，已经出现了一座白菜堆，下层三株，中层两株，顶上一株，向他叠成一个很大的 A 字。

杨译本：Beside the bookcase behind him appeared **a mound of cabbages**, three at the bottom, two above, and one at the top, confronting him like a large letter A.

（2）a sea of faces

原文：鼎里的水却一平如镜，上面浮着一层油，照出许多人脸孔：王后，王妃，武士，老臣，侏儒，太监……

杨译本：The water, now as smooth as a mirror, was coated with oil which reflected **a sea of faces**: the queen, the concubines, guards, old ministers, dwarfs, eunuchs…

三、N of N 搭配

（一）总体对比

N of N 搭配是常见的搭配。我们对比两类译本中该类搭配后发现，母语译者该类搭配使用频率高于非母语译者，统计如下：

表 10.7 母语—非母语译者译本 N of N 搭配使用统计对比

搭配	母语译者	非母语译者	蓝译本	杨译本
N of N	1870	1379	581	405

N of N 是常见的隐喻搭配。统计对比两类译本中的该类型搭配后发现，蓝译本使用 17 例该类搭配，共计 15 种；杨译本使用 8 例，共计 5 种。蓝译本中该类

搭配使用的频次与丰富度显著高于杨译本。需要说明的是,某些此类搭配与量名搭配有重合。具体对比如下表:

表 10.8 蓝译本与杨译本 N of N 搭配使用词汇对比

译本	蓝译本(15/17)	杨译本(5/8)
N of N 比喻	ashes of defeat aura of sanctity burden of falsity cocoon of loneliness dustbin of history fat beads of sweat heat of discomfort invisible walls of solitude rich tapestry of life sea of blood sea of pigtails shackles of tradition stream of consciousness thick blanket of snow tower of barley tower of barley white net of flakes	beads of sweat black tongues of flame burden of emptiness heavy burden of emptiness heavy burden of emptiness heavy burden of emptiness heavy burden of hypocrisy sea of faces

我们将该类搭配的翻译策略归类为直译与意译,直译指原文中亦为隐喻结构或者意思相近的表达,意译则指较为自由的处理。具体统计、分析如下:

表 10.9 鲁迅小说蓝译本与杨译本 N of N 搭配所涉翻译策略对比统计

搭配	蓝译本	杨译本
直译	8	6
意译	9	2
合计	17	8

(二)译例解析

1. 蓝译本中直译案例

(1)糖塔①

原文:他平日安排停当的前程,这时候又像受潮的糖塔一般,刹时倒塌,只剩下一堆碎片了。

蓝译本：Like a **tower of barley sugar** attacked by rain, his glorious future crumbled about him, leaving only fragments at his feet.

（2）糖塔②

原文：他目睹着许多东西，然而很模胡——是倒塌了的糖塔一般的前程躺在他面前。

蓝译本：Objects – a crowd of them – swam before him: his future lay before him like a crumbled **tower of barley sugar**, a monumental heap blocking his way forward.

（3）独头茧

原文："那你可错误了。人们其实并不这样。你实在亲手造了独头茧，将自己裹在里面了。你应该将世间看得光明些。"我叹惜着说。

蓝译本："Well, you're wrong," I sighed. "People aren't like that. You've spun a **cocoon of loneliness** around yourself. Can't you try to see the bright side of things?"

（4）真实的重担

原文：我没有负着虚伪的重担的勇气，却将真实的重担卸给她了。

蓝译本：Lacking the courage to bear the **burden of falsity**, I set upon her the heavier burden of the truth.

（5）旧思想的束缚

原文：这些地方，子君就大概还未脱尽旧思想的束缚……

蓝译本：I feared, at such moments, that Zijun had not yet freed herself of the **shackles of tradition**…

（6）看不见的高墙，将我隔成孤身

原文：我只觉得我四面有看不见的高墙，将我隔成孤身，使我非常气闷。

蓝译本：I was aware only of the high, suffocating, invisible **walls of solitude**.

（7）大粒的汗

原文：但是没有客人；只有小栓坐在里排的桌前吃饭，大粒的汗，从额上滚下，夹袄也帖住了脊心，两块肩胛骨高高凸出，印成一个阳文的"八"字。

蓝译本：No customers, only his son, sitting eating at one of the inner tables, fat **beads of sweat** rolling off his forehead, thick jacket stuck to his spine, the hunched ridges of his shoulder blades almost joined in an inverted V.

（8）厚厚的雪褥

原文：雪花落在积得厚厚的雪褥上面，听去似乎瑟瑟有声，使人更加感得沉寂。

蓝译本：The new flakes fell on to an already thick **blanket of snow**; if you listened out, you could even hear the rustle of their landing, sharpening the overwhelming sense of stillness.

2. 杨译本中的直译案例

（1）糖塔

原文：他平日安排停当的前程，这时候又像受潮的糖塔一般，刹时倒塌，只剩下一堆碎片了。

杨译本：Once more the future mapped out so carefully had crashed in ruins like a wet **sugar-candy pagoda**, leaving nothing but debris behind.

（2）虚空的重担①

原文：负着虚空的重担，在严威和冷眼中走着所谓人生的路，这是怎么可怕的事呵！而况这路的尽头，又不过是——连墓碑也没有的坟墓。

杨译本：How terrible to bear the heavy **burden of emptiness**, treading out one's life amid sternness and cold looks! And at the end not even a tombstone to your grave!

（3）真实的重担

原文：我没有负着虚伪的重担的勇气，却将真实的重担卸给她了。

杨译本：I hadn't the courage to shoulder the heavy **burden of hypocrisy**, so I thrust the burden of the truth on to her.

（4）虚空的重担②

原文：她虽是想在严威和冷眼中负着虚空的重担来走所谓人生的路，也已经不能。

杨译本：Although she wanted to bear the **burden of emptiness** amid sternness and cold glances till the end of her days, it had been too much for her.

（5）虚空的重担③

原文：然而子君的葬式却又在我的眼前，是独自负着<u>虚空的重担</u>，在灰白的长路上前行，而又即刻消失在周围的严威和冷眼里了。

杨译本：Then Tzu-chun's funeral springs to my mind. She bore the heavy **burden of emptiness** alone, advancing down the long grey road, only to be swallowed up amid sternness and cold glances.

（6）大粒的汗

原文：但是没有客人；只有小栓坐在里排的桌前吃饭，<u>大粒的汗</u>，从额上滚下，夹袄也帖住了脊心，两块肩胛骨高高凸出，印成一个阳文的"八"字。

杨译本：…but no customers had arrived. Only his son sat eating at a table by the wall. **Beads of sweat** stood out on his forehead, his lined jacket clung to his spine, and his shoulder blades stuck out so sharply, an inverted V seemed stamped there.

3. 蓝译本中的意译案例

（1）dustbin of history

原文：死了以后，便没有一个人再叫阿 Quei 了，那里还会有"著之竹帛"的事。

蓝译本：After his death, when he was firmly consigned to the **dustbin of history**, no one called him Ah-Quei, or indeed anything at all.

（2）ashes of defeat

原文：所以凡是和阿 Q 玩笑的人们，几乎全知道他有这一种精神上的胜利法……

蓝译本：In this way, Ah-Q's tormentors learned of his habit of declaring moral victory over the **ashes of defeat**.

（3）aura of sanctity

原文：否则，也如孔庙里的太牢一般，虽然与猪羊一样，同是畜生，但既经圣人下箸，先儒们便不敢妄动了。

蓝译本：Or maybe Ah-Q became as untouchable as the sacrificial beef in Confucius's ancestral temple – because the sage had once touched it with his scared chopsticks, it acquired an **aura of sanctity** for his disciples.

（4）tapestry of life

原文：然而他又没有全发昏，有时虽然着急，有时却也泰然；他意思之间，似乎觉得人生天地间，大约本来有时也未免要杀头的。

蓝译本：Yet he remained conscious, veering between fear, calm and the dawning sense that, in the rich **tapestry of life**, a man is destined sometimes to have his head cut off.

（5）heat of discomfort

原文：孔乙己便涨红了脸，额上的青筋条条绽出，争辩道，"窃书不能算偷……窃书！……读书人的事，能算偷么？"

蓝译本：Kong's face would flush scarlet, the veins on his forehead throbbing in the **heat of discomfort**. "Stealing books is no crime! Is scholarship theft?"

（6）sea of pigtails

原文：呵！不得了了，人言啧啧了；我却只装作不知道，一任他们光着头皮，和许多辫子一齐上讲堂。

蓝译本：Everyone was talking about it, but I had to pretend I didn't know a thing, just let them sit through my classes – the only crew-cuts in a **sea of pigtails**.

（7）stream of consciousness

原文：他想到这里，忽然从床上跳起来了。

蓝译本：He interrupted his **stream of consciousness** by leaping out of bed.

（8）net of flakes

原文：我独自向着自己的旅馆走，寒风和雪片扑在脸上，倒觉得很爽快。见天色已是黄昏,和屋宇和街道都织在密雪的纯白而不定的罗网里。

蓝译本:Alone, I walked off towards my hotel, refreshed by the wind and snow, a fine, white **net of flakes** swirling around the dusk sky, and over the buildings and street below.

(9) sea of blood

原文:彼用百头颅,千头颅兮用万头颅!我用一头颅兮而无万夫。爱一头颅兮血乎呜呼!

蓝译本:The king lets loose a **sea of blood**. I but a droplet or a stream. Yet I love this head: of blood I dream.

4. 杨译本中的意译案例

(1) black tongues of flame

原文:身子是岩石一般挺立着,眼光直射,闪闪如岩下电,须发开张飘动,像黑色火,这一瞬息,使人仿佛想见他当年射日的雄姿。

杨译本:Standing there firm as a rock, his eyes darting lightning, his beard and hair flying in the wind like **black tongues of flame**, for one instant he looked again the hero who, long ago, had shot the suns.

(2) sea of faces

原文:鼎里的水却一平如镜,上面浮着一层油,照出许多人脸孔:王后,王妃,武士,老臣,侏儒,太监……

杨译本:The water, now as smooth as a mirror, was coated with oil which reflected a **sea of faces**: the queen, the concubines, guards, old ministers, dwarfs, eunuchs...

本章小结

本章对比了鲁迅小说母语译者译本与非母语译者译本中的副动搭配、量名搭配以及 N of N 搭配情况。通过对比,发现:①两类译本中副动搭配数量接近,母语译者译本更多使用进一步修饰型副动搭配;②母语译者译本量名搭配使用更多,种类也更加丰富;③ N of N 结构在母语译者译本中使用频率更高。比较蓝译本与杨译本后发现,蓝译本中的 N of N 比喻修辞结构使用修辞频率也更多;另外,从该类搭配涉及的翻译策略上来看,蓝译本也更为丰富。

结　语

一、研究发现

本研究通过语料库方法比较、分析了汉语小说英译的母语译者与非母语译者在词汇语域、动词、名词、形容词、副词、代词、情态动词、介词、连词、词汇搭配等方面的系统性差异。基于定量的统计与定性的分析后，我们有以下发现。

（一）母语译者词汇使用更加丰富

总体而言，母语译者译本平均使用的词汇数量超过非母语译者译本（鲁迅小说两译本为例外），这在某种程度上似乎说明，母语译者在信息传递方面更加详实。而从词类数量来看，母语译者平均使用了比非母语译者更多的词类，其中，《红楼梦》、鲁迅小说以及《聊斋志异》的母语译者译本使用词类相比非母语译者译本超出幅度较大。这说明，母语译者使用的词汇更加丰富。我们对两类译本中各词性使用进行了相应的统计，发现其中也呈现相应的特征。但有一些例外情况，如《浮生六记》的林译本比拜伦译本多出359个词类。这从另一个角度说明林译本独具特色，值得更为深入的研究。

上述统计在一些更为细致的分析中得到验证。例如，对比两类译本中的言说动词、感知动词等后发现，母语译者译本中该类词汇的数量和类别平均高于非母语译者译本。

（二）母语译者词汇文体更加正式

总体而言，母语译者译本平均词长高于非母语译者译本，这说明母语译者译本的语域相对更加正式；从平均句长来看，母语译者译本均较非母语译者译本句子更长，这在某种程度上表明，母语译者译本的句式可能更为复杂。

再从各长度单词分布情况来看，非母语译者译本中长度为 3、4、5、6 字母的单词占比平均高于母语译者译本，而其他长度的单词占比低于母语译者译本。这说明，母语译者译本的词汇正式程度高于非母语译者译本。

我们通过对比鲁迅小说蓝译本与杨译本发现，蓝译本更加充分地利用了语域的文体价值，人物刻画更为生动。

（三）母语译者译本词汇情感意义更丰富

母语译者译本比非母语译者译本更多地使用情感色彩更加浓厚的词汇。例如，统计母语译者译本与非母语译者译本中表达"大"和"小"的近义形容词后发现，母语译者在表达"大"和"小"的意思时，相对非母语译者而言，会更加倾向于选择 great、tiny 和 little 等情感色彩较为浓厚的词语，而避开 big、small 等相对中性的词语。同时，母语译者还表现出对 own 等强调形容词以及用于夸张修辞的最高级形容词的偏好。此外，针对代词的研究也发现，母语译者更偏好使用情感意义更浓的指示代词结构，如 this(these) / that(those) + 双重属格；this(these) / that(those) + 隐喻结构；this(these) /that(those) + 形容词（可选）+ 名词（指人）。

（四）母语译者更偏爱抽象表达

我们统计了 5 类表达性质、状态之义的抽象名词，发现非母语译者使用的抽象名词无论在数量上还是种类上都低于母语译者，这说明母语译者对抽象性表达的偏向。

（五）母语译者更倾向避免词汇重复

我们通过对比鲁迅小说的蓝译本与杨译本对"秀才"与"举人"两个名词的英译，发现蓝译本的英译变换更为丰富多样。蓝译本共使用 11 种表达"秀才"的方式，而杨译本使用了 4 种；针对"举人"，蓝译本共有 11 种表达，而杨译本只使用了 6 种。

这种避免重复的倾向也体现在其他方面，如我们比较两类译本对原文否定意义的英译策略时，发现母语译者使用了类别更为丰富的否定结构。

(六)母语译者相对偏好使用描写类词汇

我们通过对母语译者译本与非母语译者译本形容词与副词的统计与分析,发现母语译者更偏好使用描写性更强的词汇,如描写性形容词和描写性副词。相比之下,非母语译者更多地使用程度副词。以译本中常见程度副词 very 和 so 为例,经统计,我们发现非母语译者更偏爱使用这两个高频程度副词。通过比较鲁迅小说两译本对原文高频程度副词"非常"和"极"的翻译,杨译本更多使用对等的程度副词,而蓝译本的表达手段则更具描写性。

(七)母语译者译本语篇衔接方式更为紧凑

介词性衔接比连词性衔接使得语篇更为紧凑。两类译者相比之下,母语译者更加注重使用介词,而非母语译者更多使用连词。我们统计两类译者译本关键值排前十的单词(介词与连词)后发现,母语译者译本中关键值排前十的单词均为介词,其中 of 关键值最高,其次为 around, through, about, into 等。相比之下,非母语译者译本的前十关键词中,仅有 after 和 under 为比较典型的介词,besides 兼作介词与连词,其他皆为连词。

(八)母语译者的语言特征更能体现西方思维

我们通过对反身代词 himself 的对比研究后发现,母语译者更倾向于使用反身代词的反身功能,这契合了两门语言之间的内在认知差异:英语反身代词具有提示自我概念中主客体分离的功能,而汉语没有形成专门用来表达主客二分概念的反身构式。

(九)母语译者更偏好超常表达

我们对比了母语译者译本与非母语译者译本中的副动搭配、量名搭配以及 N of N 搭配情况,发现母语译者译本更多使用进一步描述型副动搭配,其中的超常搭配也更多;在对比量词表达和 N of N 搭配时发现,母语译者使用的比喻性搭配数量更多。

(十)母语译者翻译策略更加灵活

相对而言,母语译者的翻译策略更加灵活。我们划分了 4 种翻译策略:对应、变换、显创和省略。通过多项对比，我们发现非母语译者偏向使用对应和变换策略；而母语译者译本相对更多使用显创策略。比如，蓝译本在言说动词和感知动词的翻译中比杨译本表现出更大的多样性和灵活度。

二、差异背后的可能原因

我们推测，母语译者与非母语译者在汉语小说英译中的词汇运用呈现上述差异，其原因除了在于译者个人风格，也在于母语思维与非母语思维之间的不同。母语译者的词汇选择更加接近地道的英语思维，也更具创造性。

三、研究价值

本研究的发现对于当代汉语小说如何走进英语世界，有一定的启发：①母语译者在语言使用风格方面确实与非母语译者存有一定的差异，这些风格上的差异或会影响汉语小说的英译本在英语世界的传播；②基于此，我国应招纳更多母语译者为当代汉语小说的英译事业服务；③致力于汉语小说英译的研究者不能只做宏观的文化描写，也应同时开展更多微观层面的文体研究，为汉语小说成功走进英语世界提供更加具体的方法论指导。

四、研究的局限

本研究以语料库为辅助手段，从多个维度系统比较汉译英小说母语译者与非母语译者词汇使用特征，在某种程度上，丰富了汉语小说英译的文体研究，也为汉语小说英译的评估提供一个特定的视角。笔者希望本研究的结论能对汉语小说在英语世界的传播提供一些有益的参照。

由于笔者才疏学浅，能力与精力有限，本书难免有疏漏之处：①语料规模有限。本研究所基于的语料为5本汉语小说的母语译者译本与非母语译者译本，语料达百万字词规模，在某种程度上能够支撑研究结论。不过，若有更大规模语料的统计支撑,则更为扎实可靠;②研究维度有限。本文重点考察的对象是词汇维度,覆盖了主要几类词性和几种词汇搭配,揭示了两类译者的若干词汇文体特征;研究并未涉及句法等更高层级的语法形式,也没有系统探索语篇衔接等其他语言现象。笔者希望在将来的研究中,在理论指导、语料与工具更为成熟的条件下,开展维度更为丰富的比较研究。

参考文献

Alexander, L. G. *Longman English Grammar*[M]. London: Addison-Wesley, 1988.

Bahumaid, S. Collocation in English-Arabic Translation[J]. *Babel*, 2006, 52(2), 133-152.

Baker, Mona. Corpus Linguistics and Translation Studies: Implications and Applications[J]. Baker et al. (Eds), *Text and Technology*, Philadelphia/Amsterdam: John Benjamins, 1993, 233-250.

Baker, Mona. Towards a Methodology for Investigating the Style of a Literary Translator[J]. *Target*, 2000, 12(2), 241-266.

Begagić, M. English Language Students' Productive and Receptive Knowledge of Collocations[J]. *ExELL*, 2014, 2(1), 46-67.

Benson, M., Benson, E., Ilson, R. *The BBI Combinatory Dictionary of English*（3rd edition）[W]. John Benjamins Publishing Company, 2010.

Catford, J.C. *A Linguistic Theory of Translation*[M]. Oxford: Oxford University Press, 1965.

Chukwu, U. Collocations in translation: Personal textbases to the rescue of dictionaries[J]. ASp[Online], 1997, 15-18. URL: http://asp.revues.org/2991.

Cowie, P. Phraseology(A). In R. Asher (ed). The Encyclopedia of Language and Linguistics [C]. Oxford: Pergamon, 1994, 3168-3171.

Crossley, S. A., Salsbury, T, Mcnamara, D. S. Assessing Lexical Proficiency Using Analytic Ratings: A Case for Collocation Accuracy[J], *Applied Linguistics*, 2015, 36(5), 570-590.

Hashemi, M., Azizinezhad, M., Dravishi, S. Collocation: a neglected aspect in teaching and learning EFL[J]. *Social and Behavioral Sciences*, 2012, 31, 522-525.

Hori, M. *Investigating Dickens' Style: A Collocational Analysis*[M]. Palgrave Macmillan, London, 2004.

Laviosa, S. The Corpus-based Approach: a New Paradigm in Translation Studies[J]. *Meta*, 1998, 43(4).

Leech, N. G. Leech, Mick, S. *Style in fiction Style in Fiction: A Linguistic Introduction to English Fiction*[M], Beijing: Foreign Language Teaching and Research Press, 2001.

Lodge, David. *The Art of Fiction*[M]. London: Secker & Warburg, 1992.

Martelli, A. A Corpus-based Description of English Lexical Collocations Used by Italianadvanced learners[A]. In E. Corino, C. Marello and C. Onesti (eds) Proceedings XII EURALEX International Congress[C]. Alessandria: Edizioni dell' Orso, 2006, 1005-1011.

Miyakoshi, T. Investigating ESL Learners' Lexical Collocations: The Acquisition of Verb+noun Collocations by Japanese Learners of English[D]. Honolulu: University of Hawaii, 2009.

Sinclair, J. *Corpus Concordance Collocation*[M]. London: Oxford University Press, 1991.

Sonja Tirkkonen-Condit. *Unique Items — Over- or Under-represented in Translated Language?*[M] Amsterdam/Philadelphia: John Benjamins, 2004.

Wu, S., Witten, I. H., Franken, M. Utilizing lexical data from a Web-derived corpus to expand productive collocation knowledge[J]. *ReCALL*, 2010, 22(1), 83-102.

Yan, H.S. Study on the Causes and Countermeasures of the Lexical Collocation Mistakes in College English[J]. *English Language Teaching*, 2010, 3(1), 162-165.

薄冰. 高级英语语法 [M]. 北京：世界知识出版社，2000.

曹明伦. 谈翻译中的语言变体和语域分析 [J]. 中国翻译，2007(05):87-88.

陈定安. 英汉比较与翻译（增订版）[M]. 北京：中国对外翻译出版公司，1998.

陈琳. 基于语料库的《红楼梦》说书套语英译研究[M]. 上海：上海外语教育出版社，2015.

冯庆华. 母语文化下的译者风格——《红楼梦》霍克斯闵福德英译本特色研究[M]. 上海：上海外语教育出版社，2008.

冯庆华. 思维模式下的译文词汇[M]. 上海：上海外语教育出版社，2012.

傅悦. 王熙凤对比下的刘姥姥：人物话语翻译与身份重塑研究[J]. 明清小说研究，2014（4）：233-249.

戴光荣，肖忠华. 基于自建英汉翻译语料库的翻译明晰化研究[J]. 中国翻译，2010（01）：76-80.

董琇. 译者风格形成的立体多元辩证观[D]. 上海外国语大学，2009.

何影，梁茂成. 中国英语学习者写作中副词与形容词搭配的使用特点[J]. 西安外国语大学学报，2010（03）：105-107.

胡开宝. 语料库翻译学：内涵与意义[J]. 外国语，2012（05）：59-70.

胡显耀. 基于语料库的汉语翻译语体特征多维分析[J]. 外语教学与研究，2010（06）：451-458，481.

胡显耀，曾佳. 翻译小说"被"字句的频率、结构及语义韵研究[J]. 外国语，2010（03）：73-79.

胡显耀，曾佳. 用语料库考察汉语翻译小说定语的容量和结构[J]. 解放军外国语学院学报，2009（03）：61-66.

黄立波. 《骆驼祥子》三个英译本中叙述话语的翻译——译者风格的语料库考察[J]. 解放军外国语学院学报，2014（01）：72-80，99.

黄立波. 基于双语平行语料库的翻译文体学探讨——以《骆驼祥子》两个英译本中人称代词主语和叙事视角转换为例[J]. 中国外语，2011（06）：100-106.

黄立波. 中国现当代小说汉英平行语料库：研制与应用[J]. 外语教学，2013（06）：104-109.

侯羽, 刘泽权, 刘鼎甲. 基于语料库的葛浩文译者风格分析——以莫言小说英译本为例 [J]. 外语与外语教学, 2014（02）: 72-78.

贾光茂. 英汉反身代词概念基础对比研究 [J]. 外语与外语教学, 2020（02）: 60-68, 148.

蒋和舟. 英汉名词回指形式对比分析 [J]. 四川外语学院学报, 2007（06）: 97-100.

姜静楠. 后现代小说中的人物 [J]. 文艺评论, 2000（02）: 16-19.

李珊妮, 贾卉. 基于语料库的中译英翻译显化共性考察——以小说《受活》为例 [J]. 江苏外语教学研究, 2016（01）: 75-80.

李雅轩. 基于语料库的葛浩文译者风格考察——以《红高粱》英译文本为例 [D]. 山东大学.

李震红. 试论英语肯定表达与汉语否定表达的互译趋势 [J]. 苏州大学学报（哲学社会科学版）, 2008（03）: 89-92.

连淑能. 英汉对比研究 [M]. 北京: 高等教育出版社, 2010.

缪佳, 邵斌. 基于语料库的英语译文语言特征与翻译共性研究——以余华小说《兄弟》英译本为个案 [J]. 天津外国语大学学报, 2014（01）: 43-49.

刘克强.《水浒传》四英译本翻译特征多维度对比研究 [D]. 上海外国语大学, 2013.

刘璇.《浮生六记》林译本的译者风格研究 [D]. 四川外国语大学, 2014.

刘泽权, 刘超朋, 朱虹.《红楼梦》四个英译本的译者风格初探——基于语料库的统计与分析 [J]. 中国翻译, 2011（01）: 60-64.

刘泽权, 田璐.《红楼梦》叙事标记语及其英译——基于语料库的对比分析 [J]. 外语学刊, 2009（01）: 106-110.

刘泽权, 闫继苗. 基于语料库的译者风格与翻译策略研究——以《红楼梦》中报道动词及英译为例 [J]. 解放军外国语学院学报, 2010（04）: 89-94, 130.

刘泽权, 张丹丹. 基于平行语料库的汉英文学翻译研究与词典编纂——以《红楼梦》"吃"熟语及其英译为例 [J]. 中国翻译, 2012（06）: 18-22.

卢静. 基于语料库的译者风格综合研究模式探索——以《聊斋志异》译本为例[J]. 外语电化教学, 2013(02): 53-58.

彭发胜, 万颖婷. 基于语料库的《边城》三个英译本文体特色分析[J]. 合肥工业大学学报(社会科学版), 2014(06): 83-89.

秦洪武, 王克非. 基于语料库的翻译语言分析——以so...that的汉语对应结构为例[J]. 现代外语, 2004(01): 40-48, 105-106.

秦洪武. 英译汉翻译语言的结构容量: 基于多译本语料库的研究[J]. 外国语, 2010(04): 73-80.

秦静, 任晓霏. 基于语料库的《红楼梦》叙事翻译研究——以主述位理论为视角[J]. 明清小说研究, 2015(04): 229-248.

沈家煊. 英汉介词对比[J]. 外语教学与研究, 1984(02): 1-8.

司炳月, 霍跃红. 基于语料库的翻译文体学视角下译者的情感指纹研究——基于态度立场标记的自建语料库研究[J]. 外语电化教学, 2014(02): 55-60.

宋庆伟, 匡华, 吴建平. 国内语料库翻译学20年述评(1993—2012)[J]. 上海翻译, 2013(02): 25-29.

孙会军. 中国小说翻译过程中的文学性再现与中国文学形象重塑[J]. 外国语文, 2018(05): 12-15.

谭业升. 译者的意象图式与合成概念化——基于语料库方法的《红楼梦》"社会脸"翻译研究[J]. 外语与外语教学, 2013(03): 55-59.

王海华, 陈国华. 中国学习者使用英语强势词搭配的发展特点[J]. 外国语, 2007(01): 52-28.

王磊. 隐喻与翻译: 一项关于《围城》英译本的个案调查[J]. 中国翻译, 2007(03): 75-79.

王克非, 胡显耀. 汉语文学翻译中人称代词的显化和变异[J]. 中国外语, 2010(04): 16-21.

王青, 秦洪武. 基于语料库的《尤利西斯》汉译词汇特征研究[J]. 外语学刊, 2011

（01）：123-127.

王瑞, 黄立波. 贾平凹小说译入译出风格的语料库考察[J]. 中国外语, 2015（004）: 97-105.

吴怀仁. 论小说写作中人物刻画的三种形态（上）[J]. 写作, 2009（04）: 20-22.

吴建. 小说翻译评估的两种文体视角[J]. 南京邮电大学学报（社会科学版）, 2017,（04）: 104-110.

武光军. 2010. 基于语料库的汉译英中的搭配教学[J]. 中国外语, 2010（04）: 53-59.

武光军, 王克非. 基于英语类比语料库的翻译文本中的搭配特征研究[J]. 中国外语, 2011（05）: 40-47, 56.

辛克莱, 约翰. 高级英语用法词典[W]. 上海: 上海外语教育出版社, 2007.

肖忠华, 戴光荣. 寻求"第三语码"——基于汉语译文语料库的翻译共性研究[J]. 外语教学与研究, 2010（01）: 52-58, 81.

徐剑英, 承云, 欧阳美和. 英汉词汇衔接与文本解读[J]. 南昌大学学报（人文社会科学版）, 2005（01）: 139-142.

严苡丹. 基于语料库的译者翻译策略研究——以《红楼梦》乔利译本中母系亲属称谓语的翻译为例[J]. 外语电化教学, 2011（05）: 67-72.

严苡丹. 《红楼梦》亲属称谓语的英译研究[M]. 上海: 上海外语教育出版社, 2012.

严苡丹, 韩宁. 基于语料库的译者风格研究——以鲁迅小说两个英译本为例[J]. 外语教学, 2015（02）: 109-113.

杨惠中. 语料库语言学导论[M]. 上海: 上海外语教育出版社, 2002.

杨柳川. 满纸"红"言译如何——霍克思《红楼梦》"红"系颜色词的翻译策略[J]. 红楼梦学刊, 2014（05）: 196-215.

姚琴. 基于平行语料库的《红楼梦》意义显化翻译考察——以霍译本林黛玉人物特征为例[J]. 外语教学与研究, 2013（03）: 453-463, 481.

张道真. 实用英语语法[M]. 北京: 外语教学与研究出版社, 2002.

赵朝永.《红楼梦》邦斯尔译本体例风格探析[J]. 现代语文（语言研究版）, 2014

(10): 130-132.

赵彦春, 吕丽荣. 中华文化"走出去": 汉籍经典英译的文学性要求——以外文出版社《道德经》英译本为例 [J]. 外语教学, 2019(06): 82-86.

朱冬青. 汉译英文本中的语义韵研究 [D]. 大连外国语大学, 2014.

后 记

　　酝酿数载,耕耘一年,终于完成书稿,交付出版,心中一块大石落地。感慨之余,想起有诸多师友亲人需要郑重感谢。

　　首先感谢我的恩师,上海外国语大学的冯庆华教授。2013年,我有幸入冯老师门下学习翻译。冯老师对《红楼梦》的热爱令我动容。他爱读红楼,喜欢谈红楼,还醉心钻研《红楼梦》的翻译问题。求学期间,冯老师主要给我们讲授两门课:一是《语料库翻译研究》;二是《<红楼梦>翻译研究》。他用语料库的方法探索《红楼梦》霍克斯和杨宪益、戴乃迭译本的译者风格,着重发掘霍克斯这位母语译者的语言风格,这给我了莫大的启发。我的这项研究承载了冯老师的教诲。

　　用语料库的方法研究译者风格确实是一块土壤肥沃的新大陆。但想要有收获,得先开垦出一亩三分地来。语料库研究方法虽好,但建设语料库,尤其是建设对照语料库是一项十分耗时费力的工作。好在我有一群聪明、勤奋的研究生帮忙。我也给他们开设了《语料库与翻译》课程,教授他们如何做语料对齐,如何进行检索,如何开展研究。他们很快就成了熟手,也成了我的得力帮手。不久后,包含5部汉语小说及其英译本的平行语料库建成了。有了现成的语料库,我们可以做更深入的探索,讨论各种潜在的研究选题和方法的可行性,师生皆有所获,真可谓教学相长。我在这里要特意感谢王梦婷、万钧儒、曲凯、高倩倩、牛倩倩、施赛男、沈晨、秦文静等研究生。

　　感谢我的妻子和两位宝贝女儿。过去的一年,我因为赶书稿的进度,对她们难免照顾不周。好在我的妻子贤惠能干,女儿乖巧可爱,并没有埋怨我。感谢我的岳父、岳母在生活上也给了我们莫大的帮助,让我得以更加专心地投入工作。

　　最后,感谢所有给过我启发和帮助的学界前辈和同仁们。如若本书的出版能对汉语小说英译研究带来哪怕一点点助益,我也深感欣慰。

吴　建
2021年6月